NEW ADVANCES IN IMAGE FUSION

Edited by **Qiguang Miao**

New Advances in Image Fusion

http://dx.doi.org/10.5772/3382
Edited by Qiguang Miao

Contributors

Dong Jiang, Hemissi Selim, Farah Imed Riadh, Md Anowar Hossain, Ibrahim Elshafiey, Majeed A. S. Alkanhal, Hina Pande, Poonam S. Tiwari, Yufeng Zheng, Wenjie Dong, Genshe Chen, Erik P. Blasch, Chen, Qiguang Miao

Published by InTech

Janeza Trdine 9, 51000 Rijeka, Croatia

Publishing Process Manager Sandra Bakic
Typesetting InTech DTP Team
Cover InTech Design Team

Additional hard copies can be obtained from orders@intechopen.com

New Advances in Image Fusion, Edited by Qiguang Miao
p. cm.
ISBN 978-953-51-1206-8

For EU product safety concerns:
IN TECH d.o.o., Prolaz Marije Krucifikse Kozulić 3, 51000 Rijeka, Croatia,
info@intechopen.com or visit our website at intechopen.com.

Meet the editor

Qiguang Miao is a professor and Ph.D. supervisor of School of Computer Science and Technology in Xidian University. In 2012, he was supported by the Program for New Century Excellent Talents in University by Ministry of Education. He received his doctor degree in computer application technology from Xidian University in December 2005. In the field of teaching, he was awarded as one of Pacemaker of Ten Excellent Teacher twice in 2008 and 2011. His research interests include machine learning, intelligent image processing and malware behavior analysis and understanding. As principal investigator, he is doing or has completed 3 projects of NSFC, 2 projects of Shaanxi provincial natural science fund, more than 10 projects of National Defence Pre-research Foundation, 863 and Weapons and Equipment fund. He has published over 50 papers in the significant domestic and international journal or conference.

Contents

Preface

Image Fusion is an important branch of information fusion, and it is also an important technology for image understanding and computer vision. The fusion process is to merging different images into one to get more accurate description for the scene. The original images for image fusion are always obtained by several different image sensors, or the same sensor in different operating modes. The fused image can provide more effective information for further image processing, such as image segmentation, object detection and recognition. Image fusion is a new study field which combined with many different disciplines, such as sensors, signal processing, image processing, computer and artificial intelligence.

Since the 1990s, image fusion has been applied in many fields, such as remote sensing, robot vision, medical imaging and diagnostics. Hence its application values are increasingly concerned by many scholars. In the past two decades, a large number of research literatures appear. This book is edited based on these research results, and many research scholars give a great help to this book.

This book consists of seven chapters. Chapter 1 introduces the applications of multi-spectral image for remote sensing techniques. This chapter is written by Dong Jiang, Dafang Zhuang, et al. These chapters focus on the multi-spectral image fusion, and several traditional and improved algorithms are present.

Chapter 2 introduces a multi-features fusion of multi-temporal hyperspectral images via a cooperative GDD/SVM method. This chapter is written by Selim Hemissi and Imed Riadh Farah. This chapter mainly discusses the feature fusion for hyperspectral data. Several feature extraction and classification algorithms are discussed in this chapter.

Chapter 3 gives a novel image fusion algorithm based wide-swath and high-resolution synthetic aperture radar system using MIMO UWB-OFDM architecture. This chapter is written by Md Anowar Hossain, Ibrahim Elshafiey, et al.

Multiple-Input Multiple-Output (MIMO) radar has been gradually concerned by people. However, only few scholars study the fusion technology on MIMO synthetic aperture radar (SAR). This chapter gives different fusion algorithms for the multi-sensor and multi-frequency imagery to enhance the resolution of the SAR image.

Chapter 4 introduces the high-resolution and hyperspectral data fusion and classification. This chapter is written by Hina Pande and Poonam S. Tiwari. High-resolution image has a high spatial resolution, and hyperspectral data has a large number of measured wavelength bands. The purpose of the fusion is to get a new image which has the spatial resolution of the high resolution image and preserves the spectral characteristics of the hyperspectral image. Several algorithms is introduced to achieve this goal, and many classification results based on the fused images are present in this chapter.

Chapter 5 introduces a new metric for objective evaluation of night vision colorization. This charter is written by Yufeng Zheng. Evaluation metric is to balance whether the fused image is good or not. This chapter mainly focuses on how to objectively evaluate the image qualities of colorized images. In this chapter, some colorization techniques are introduced, and a new colorization metric, OEI, is proposed.

Chapter 6 shows the application of à trous wavelet in image fusion. à trous wavelet has the shift-invariance, and it has a better property than Mallat wavelet. Hence it is more suitable for image fusion. In this chapter, the theory of à trous wavelet is introduced, and several test experiments are shown.

Chapter 7 introduces the image fusion algorithm via shearlets. This chapter is written by Miao Qiguang, Shi Cheng, et al. Shearlet was proposed in 2005. In this chapter, the theory of shearlet is introduced. Meanwhile, for the multi-focus image, a novel fusion framework based on shearlets is proposed. And for the remote sensing image, combined with PCNN, a new fusion algorithm is discussed.

This book focus on the latest research achievements, and to some extent reflects the current work of the scholars. Thanks to all the scholars who have contributed to this book.

Prof. Qiguang Miao
School of Computer Science and Technology
Xidian University
China

Chapter 1

Investigation of Image Fusion for Remote Sensing Application

Dong Jiang, Dafang Zhuang and Yaohuan Huang

Additional information is available at the end of the chapter

http://dx.doi.org/10.5772/56946

1. Introduction

Remote sensing techniques have proven to be powerful tools for the monitoring of the Earth's surface and atmosphere on a global, regional, and even local scale, by providing important coverage, mapping and classification of land cover features such as vegetation, soil, water and forests. The volume of remote sensing images continues to grow at an enormous rate due to advances in sensor technology for both high spatial and temporal resolution systems. Consequently, an increasing quantity of image data from airborne/satellite sensors have been available, including multi-resolution images, multi-temporal images, multi-frequency/spectral bands images and multi-polarization image. Remote sensing information is convenient and easy to be accessed over a large area at low cost, but due to the impact of cloud, aerosol, solar elevation angle and bio-directional reflection, the surface energy parameters retrieved from remote sensing data are often missing; meanwhile, the seasonal variation of surface parameter time-series plots will be also affected. To reduce such impacts, generally time composite method is adopted. The goal of multiple sensor data fusion is to integrate complementary and redundant information to provide a composite image which could be used to better understanding of the entire scene.

1.1. Definition of image fusion

The definition of image fusion varies. For example:

- *Image fusion is the combination of two or more different images to form a new image by using a certain algorithm (Genderen and Pohl 1994) [1].*

- *Image fusion is the process of combining information from two or more images of a scene into a single composite image that is more informative and is more suitable for visual perception or computer processing. (Guest editorial of Information Fusion, 2007) [2].*
- *Image fusion is a process of combining images, obtained by sensors of different wavelengths simultaneously viewing of the same scene, to form a composite image. The composite image is formed to improve image content and to make it easier for the user to detect, recognize, and identify targets and increase his situational awareness. 2010. (http://www.hcltech.com/aerospace-and-defense/ enhanced-vision-system/).*

Image fusion has proved to be an effective way for optimum utilization of large volumes of image from multiple sources since early 1990's. Multiple image fusion seeks to combine information from multiple sources to achieve inferences that are not feasible from a single sensor or source. It is the aim of image fusion to integrate different data in order to obtain more information than can be derived from each of the single sensor data alone [3].

This chapter focused on multi-sensor image fusion in remote sensing. The fusion of information from sensors with different physical characteristics enhances the understanding of our surroundings and provides the basis for regional planning, decision-making, urban sprawl monitoring and land use/ land cover classification, etc.

1.2. Techniques and application of image fusion

In the past decades it has been applied to different fields such as pattern recognition, visual enhancement, object detection and area surveillance.In 1997, Hall and Llinas gave a general introduction to multi-sensor data fusion [4]. Another in-depth review paper on multiple sensors data fusion techniques was published in 1998 [3]. This paper explained the concepts, methods and applications of image fusion as a contribution to multi-sensor integration oriented data processing. Since then, image fusion has received increasing attention. Further scientific papers on image fusion have been published with an emphasis on improving fusion quality and finding more application areas. As a case in point, Simone *et al.* describe three typical applications of data fusion in remote sensing, such as obtaining elevation maps from synthetic aperture radar (SAR) interferometers, the fusion of multi-sensor and multi-temporal images, and the fusion of multi-frequency, multi-polarization and multi-resolution SAR images [5]. Quite a few survey papers have been published recently, providing overviews of the history, developments, and the current state of the art of image fusion in the image-based application fields [6-8], but recent development of multi-sensor data fusion in remote sensing fields has not been discussed in detail (Table 1).

2. Advance in image fusion techniques

2.1. Categorization of image fusion techniques

During the past two decades, several fusion techniques have been proposed. Most of these techniques are based on the compromise between the desired spatial enhancement and the

Data source	Objective	Authors	Time
SPOT HRV & ERS SAR	Automatic registration	Olivier Thepaut, Kidiyo Kpalma, Joseph Ronsin [9]	1994
Hyperspectral image & SAR image	Automatic target cueing	Tamar Peli, Mon Young, Robert Knox, Ken Ellis, Fredrick Bennet [10]	1999
Multifrequency, multipolarization SAR images	Land use classification	G. Simone, A. Farina, F.C. Morabito, S.B. Serpico, L. Bruzzone [5]	2001
Landsat ETM+ Pan band & CBERS-1 multiple spectral data	Methods comparison	Marcia L.S. Aguena, Nelson D.A. Mascarenhas [11]	2006
Landsat ETM+ & MODIS	Urban sprawl monitoring	Ying Lei, Dong Jiang, and Xiaohuan Yang [12]	2007
AVIRIS and LIDAR	Coastal mapping	Ahmed F. Elaksher [13]	2008

Table 1. Examples of application of image fusion

spectral consistency. Among the hundreds of variations of image fusion techniques, the widely used methods include, but are not limited to, intensity-hue-saturation (IHS), high-pass filtering, principal component analysis (PCA), different arithmetic combination(e.g. Brovey transform), multi-resolution analysis-based methods (e.g. pyramid algorithm, wavelet transform), and Artificial Neural Networks (ANNs), etc. The chapter will provide a general introduction to those selected methods with emphases on new advances in the remote sensing field. In general, all above mentioned approaches can be divided into four different types: signal level, pixel level, feature level, and decision level image fusion [4].

1. Signal level fusion. In signal-based fusion, signals from different sensors are combined to create a new signal with a better signal-to noise ratio than the original signals.

2. Pixel level fusion. Pixel-based fusion is performed on a pixel-by-pixel basis. It generates a fused image in which information associated with each pixel is determined from a set of pixels in source images to improve the performance of image processing tasks such as segmentation

3. Feature level fusion. Feature-based fusion at feature level requires an extraction of objects recognized in the various data sources. It requires the extraction of salient features which are depending on their environment such as pixel intensities, edges or textures. These similar features from input images are fused.

4. Decision-level fusion consists of merging information at a higher level of abstraction, combines the results from multiple algorithms to yield a final fused decision. Input im-

ages are processed individually for information extraction. The obtained information is then combined applying decision rules to reinforce common interpretation.

2.2. Advance in image fusion methods

2.2.1. Convenient image fusion methods

The PCA transform converts inter-correlated multi-spectral (MS) bands into a new set of uncorrelated components. To do this approach first we must get the principle components of the MS image bands. After that, the first principle component which contains the most information of the image is substituted by the panchromatic image. Finally the inverse principal component transform is done to get the new RGB (Red, Green, and Blue) bands of multi-spectral image from the principle components.

The IHS fusion converts a color MS image from the RGB space into the IHS color space. Because the intensity (I) band resembles a panchromatic (PAN) image, it is replaced by a high-resolution PAN image in the fusion. A reverse IHS transform is then performed on the PAN together with the hue (H) and saturation (S) bands, resulting in an IHS fused image.

Different arithmetic combinations have been developed for image fusion. The Brovey transform, Synthetic Variable Ratio (SVR), and Ratio Enhancement (RE) techniques are some successful examples. The basic procedure of the Brovey transform first multiplies each MS band by the high resolution PAN band, and then divides each product by the sum of the MS bands. The SVR and RE techniques are similar, but involve more sophisticated calculations for the MS sum for better fusion quality.

Convenient fusion algorithms mentioned above have been widely used for relatively simple and time efficient fusion schemes. However, several problems must be considered before their application: 1) These fusion algorithms generate a fused image from a set of pixels in the various sources. These pixel-level fusion methods are very sensitive to registration accuracy, so that co-registration of input images at sub-pixel level is required; 2) One of the main limitations of HIS and Brovey transform is that the number of input multiple spectral bands should be equal or less than three at a time; 3) These image fusion methods are often successful at improves the spatial resolution, however, they tend to distort the original spectral signatures to some extent [14, 15]. More recently new techniques such as the wavelet transform seem to reduce the color distortion problem and to keep the statistical parameters invariable.

2.2.2. Multi-resolution analysis-based methods

Multi-resolution or multi-scale methods, such as pyramid transformation, have been adopted for data fusion since the early 1980s [16]. The Pyramid-based image fusion methods, including Laplacian pyramid transform, were all developed from Gaussian pyramid transform, have been modified and widely used [17, 18].

In 1989, Mallat put all the methods of wavelet construction into the framework of functional analysis and described the fast wavelet transform algorithm and general method of constructing wavelet orthonormal basis. On the basis, wavelet transform can be really applied to image decomposition and reconstruction [19, 20]. Wavelet transforms provide a framework in which an image is decomposed, with each level corresponding to a coarser resolution band. For example, in the case of fusing a MS image with a high-resolution PAN image with wavelet fusion, the Pan image is first decomposed into a set of low-resolution Pan images with corresponding wavelet coefficients (spatial details) for each level. Individual bands of the MS image then replace the low-resolution Pan at the resolution level of the original MS image. The high resolution spatial detail is injected into each MS band by performing a reverse wavelet transform on each MS band together with the corresponding wavelet coefficients (Figure 1).

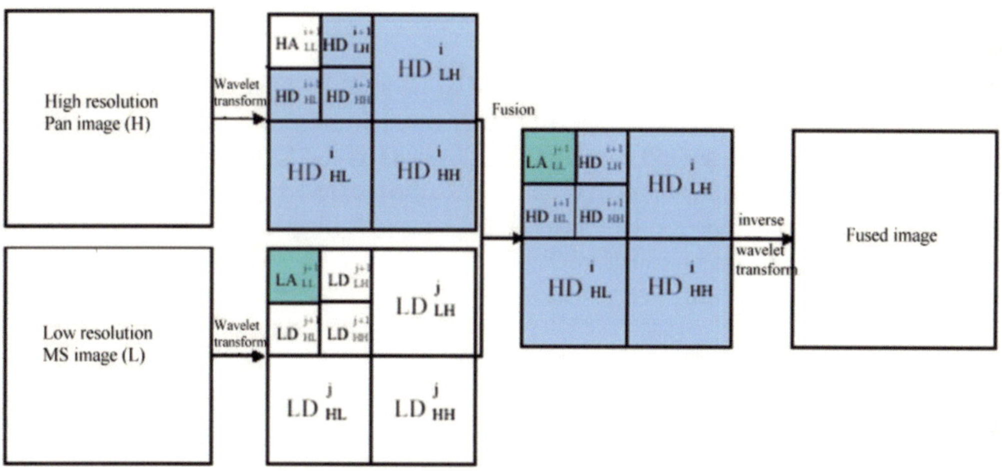

Figure 1. Generic flowchart of wavelet-based image fusion

In the wavelet-based fusion schemes, detail information is extracted from the PAN image using wavelet transforms and injected into the MS image. Distortion of the spectral information is minimized compared to the standard methods. In order to achieve optimum fusion results, various wavelet-based fusion schemes had been tested by many researchers. Among these schemes several new concepts/algorithms were presented and discussed. Candes provided a method for fusing SAR and visible MS images using the Curvelet transformation. The method was proven to be more efficient for detecting edge information and denoising than wavelet transformation [21]. Curvelet-based image fusion has been used to merge a Landsat ETM+ panchromatic and multiple-spectral image. The proposed method simultaneously provides richer information in the spatial and spectral domains [22]. Donoho *et al.* presented a flexible multi-resolution, local, and directional image expansion using contour segments, the Contourlet transform, to solve the problem that wavelet transform could not efficiently represent the singularity of linear/curve in image processing [23]. Contourlet transform provides flexible number of directions and captures the intrinsic geometrical structure of images.

In general, as a typical feature level fusion method, wavelet-based fusion could evidently perform better than convenient methods in terms of minimizing color distortion and denoising effects. It has been one of the most popular fusion methods in remote sensing in recent years, and has been standard module in many commercial image processing soft wares, such as ENVI, PCI, ERDAS. Problems and limitations associated with them include: (1) Its computational complexity compared to the standard methods; (2) Spectral content of small objects often lost in the fused images; (3) It often requires the user to determine appropriate values for certain parameters (such as thresholds). The development of more sophisticated wavelet-based fusion algorithm (such as Ridgelet, Curvelet, and Contourlet transformation) could improve the performance results, but these new schemes may cause greater complexity in the computation and setting of parameters.

2.2.3. Artificial neural network based fusion method

Artificial neural networks (ANNs) have proven to be a more powerful and self-adaptive method of pattern recognition as compared to traditional linear and simple nonlinear analyses [24]. The ANN-based method employs a nonlinear response function that iterates many times in a special network structure in order to learn the complex functional relationship between input and output training data. The general schematic diagram of the ANN-based image fusion method can be seen in Figure 2.

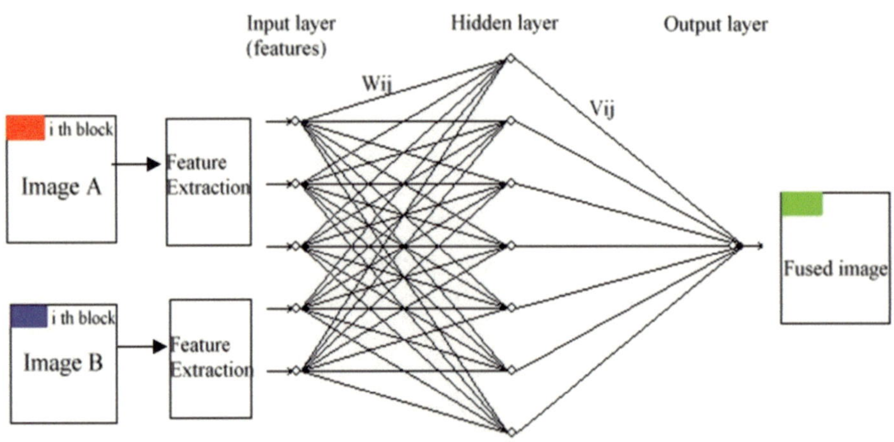

Figure 2. General schematic diagram of the ANN-based image fusion method.

The input layer has several neurons, which represent the feature factors extracted and normalized from image A and image B. The function of each neuron is a sigmoid function given by [25]:

$$f(x) = \frac{1}{1+e^{-x}} \tag{1}$$

In Figure 6, the hidden layer has several neurons and the output layer has one neuron (or more neuron). The *i*th neuron of the input layer connects with the *j*th neuron of the hidden layer by weight W_{ij}, and weight between the *j*th neuron of the hidden layer and the *t*th neuron of output layer is V_{jt} (in this case $t = 1$). The weighting function is used to simulate and recognize the response relationship between features of fused image and corresponding feature from original images (image A and image B). The ANN model is given as follows:

$$Y = \frac{1}{1 + \exp\left[-\left(\sum_{j=1}^{q} V_j H_j - \gamma\right)\right]} \tag{2}$$

In equation (6), Y=pixel value of fused image exported from the neural network model, q=number of nodes hidden (q~8 here), V_j=weight between *j*th hidden node and output node (in this case, there is only one output node), c=threshold of the output node, H_j=exported values from the *j*th hidden node:

$$H = \frac{1}{1 + \exp\left[-\left(\sum_{i=1}^{n} W_{ij} a_i - \theta_j\right)\right]} \tag{3}$$

Where W_{ij}=weight between *i*th input node and the *j*th hidden node, a_i=values of the *i*th input factor, n=number of nodes of input (n~5 here), h_j=threshold of the *j*th hidden node.

As the first step of ANN-based data fusion, two registered images are decomposed into several blocks with size of M and N (Figure 2). Then, features of the corresponding blocks in the two original images are extracted, and the normalized feature vector incident to neural networks can be constructed. The features used here to evaluate the fusion effect are normally spatial frequency, visibility, and edge. The next step is to select some vector samples to train neural networks. An ANN is a universal function approximator that directly adapts to any nonlinear function defined by a representative set of training data. Once trained, the ANN model can remember a functional relationship and be used for further calculations. For these reasons, the ANN concept has been adopted to develop strongly nonlinear models for multiple sensors data fusion. Thomas *et al.* discussed the optimal fusion method of TV and infrared images using artificial neural networks [26]. After that, many neural network models have been proposed for image fusion such as BP, SOFM, and ARTMAP neural networks. BP algorithm has been mostly used. However, the convergence of BP networks is slow and the global minima of the error space may not be always achieved [27]. As an unsupervised network, SOFM network clusters input sample through competitive learning. But the number of output neurons should be set before constructing neural networks model [28]. RBF neural network can approximate objective function at any precise level if enough hidden units are provided. The advantages of RBF network training include no iteration, few training parameters, high training speed, simply process and memory functions [29]. Hong explored the way that using RBF neural networks combined with nearest neighbor clustering method to cluster, and membership weighting is used to fuse. Experiments show this method can obtain the better effect of cluster fusion with proper width parameter [30].

Gail *et al.* used Adaptive Resonance Theory (ART) neural networks to form a new framework for self-organizing information fusion. The ARTMAP neural network can act as a self-organizing expert system to derive hierarchical knowledge structures from inconsistent training data [31]. ARTMAP information fusion resolves apparent contradictions in input pixel labels by assigning output classes to levels in a knowledge hierarchy. Wang *et al.* presented a feature-level image fusion method based on segmentation region and neural networks. The results indicated that this combined fusion scheme was more efficient than that of traditional methods [32].

The ANN-based fusion method exploits the pattern recognition capabilities of artificial neural networks, and meanwhile, the learning capability of neural networks makes it feasible to customize the image fusion process. Many of applications indicated that the ANN-based fusion methods had more advantages than traditional statistical methods, especially when input multiple sensor data were incomplete or with much noises. It is often served as an efficient decision level fusion tools for its self learning characters, especially in land use/land cover classification. In addition, the multiple inputs – multiple outputs framework make it to be a possible approach to fuse high dimension data, such as long-term time-series data or hyper-spectral data.

2.2.4. Dempster-Shafer evidence theory based fusion method

Dempster-Shafer decision theory is considered a generalized Bayesian theory, used when the data contributing to the determination of the analysis of the images is subject to uncertainty. It allows distributing support for proposition not only to a proposition itself but also to the union of propositions that include it. Huadong Wu et.al. presented a system framework that manages information overlap and resolves conflicts, and the system provides eneralizable architectural support that facilitates sensor fusion [33].

Compared with Bayesian theory, the Dempster-Shafer theory of evidence feels closer to our human perception and reasoning processes. Its capability to assign uncertainty or ignorance to propositions is a powerful tool for dealing with a large range of problems that otherwise would seem intractable [33]. The Dempster-Shafer theory of evidence has been applied on image fusion using SPOT/HRV image and NOAA/AVHRR series. The results show unambiguously the major improvement brought by such a data fusion, and the performance of the proposed method [34]. H. Borotschnig et.al. compared three frameworks for information fusion and view-planning using different uncertainty calculi: probability theory, possibility theory and Dempster-Shafer theory of evidence [35]. The results indicated that Dempster-Shafer decision theory based sensor fusion method will achieve much higher performance improvement, and it provides estimates of imprecision and uncertainty of the information derived from different sources

3. Applications of image fusion

It has been widely used in many fields of remote sensing, such as object identification, classification, and change detection. The following paragraphs describe the recent achievements of image fusion in more detail.

3.1. Object identification

The feature enhancement capability of image fusion is visually apparent in VIR/VIR combinations that often results in images that are superior to the original data. In order to maximize the amount of information extracted from satellite image data useful products can be found in fused images [3]. An integrated system for automatic road mapping from high-resolution multi-spectral satellite imagery by information fusion was discussed by Jin *et al.* in 2005 [36]. Garzeli. A. presents a solution to enhance the spatial resolution of MS images with high-resolution PAN data. The proposed method exploits the undecimated discrete wavelet transform, and the vector multi-scale Kalman filter, which is used to model the injection process of wavelet details. Fusion simulations on spatially degraded data and fusion tests at the full scale reveal that an accurate and reliable PAN-sharpening is achieved by the proposed method [37]. A case study, which extracted artificial forest and residential areas using high spatial resolution image and multiple spectral images, was shown as follows.

Forest classification and mapping provides an important basis for forest monitoring and ecological protection. The method based on single pixel or only on spectral features cannot effectively distinguish the types of forest. Here we present an approach for extracted artificial forest areas using SPOT 5 Panchromatic band and multiple spectral images in Naban River National Nature Reserve, is located in Jing Hong City, Yunnan province, South China. The resolution of the panchromatic band of SPOT-5 image is 2.5 m and that of the multispectral bands is 10 m. The Pansharpening fusion method is first used for panchromatic and multi-spectral data fusion of SPOT-5 image data. Next, histogram equalization, median filtering and PCA method are used to make image optical spectrum enhancement and denoising, so as to improve the multi-scale image segmentation effect. Compared with the original spectrum data, the image textures of artificial forest after the pretreatment are regularly arranged and its visual texture features are very obvious. The particle size information of natural forests is significant. So that forest classification could be easily achieved (Figure 3).

3.2. Land use and land cover classification

Classification of land use and land cover is one of the key tasks of remote sensing applications. The classification accuracy of remote sensing images is improved when multiple source image data are introduced to the processing [3]. Images from microwave and optical sensors offer complementary information that helps in discriminating the different classes. As discussed in the work of Wu *et al.*, a multi-sensor decision level image fusion algorithm based on fuzzy theory are used for classification of each sensor image, and the classification results are fused by the fusion rule. Interesting result was achieved mainly for the high speed classification and efficient fusion of complementary information [38]. Land-use/land-

Figure 3. Extracted artificial forest and residential areas using image fusion techniques; (a) Before fusion (Artificial forest), (b) Fused image (Artificial forest), (c) Before fusion (Natural forest), (d) Fused image (Natural forest and residential area)and residential area.

cover classification had been improved using data fusion techniques such as ANN and the Dempster-Shafer theory of evidence. The experimental results show that the excellent performance of classification as compared to existing classification techniques [39, 40]. Image fusion methods will lead to strong advances in land use/land cover classifications by use of the complementary of the data presenting either high spatial resolution or high time repetitiveness.

For example, Indian P5 Panchromatic image(Figure 4 b) with spatial resolution of 2.18 m of Yiwu City, Southeast China, in 2007 was fused with multiple spectral bands of China-Brazil CBERS data (spatial resolution: 19.2m) (Figure 4 a)in 2007. Brovey transformation fusion method was used.

Figure 4. Result of image fusion: CBERS MS and P5 PAN; (a) CBERS multiple spectral image (b) Fused image

Figure 5. Different land use types in fused image; (a) cultivated land (b) water (c) urban settlements

Results indicated that the accuracy of residential areas of Yiwu city derived from fused image is much higher than result derived from CBERS multiple spectral image (Figure 5).

3.3. Change detection

Change detection is the process of identifying differences in the state of an object or phenomenon by observing it at different times. Change detection is an important process in monitoring and managing natural resources and urban development because it provides quantitative analysis of the spatial distribution of the population of interest [41]. Image fusion for change detection takes advantage of the different configurations of the platforms carrying the sensors. The combination of these temporal images in same place enhances information on changes that might have occurred in the area observed. Sensor image data with low temporal resolution and high spatial resolution can be fused with high temporal resolution data to enhance the changing information of certain ground objects. Madhavan *et al.* presented a decision level fusion system that automatically performs fusion of information from multi-spectral, multi-resolution, and multi-temporal high-resolution airborne data for a change-detection analysis. Changes are automatically detected in buildings, building structures, roofs, roof color, industrial structures, smaller vehicles, and vegetation [42]. An example of change detection using Landsat ETM+ and MODIS data is presented as follow.

Recent study indicated that urban expansion could be efficiently monitored using satellite images with multi-temporal and multi-spatial resolution. For example, Landsat ETM+ Panchromatic image(Figure 6 a) with spatial resolution of 10 m of Chongqing City, Southwest China, in 2000 was fused with daily-received multiple spectral bands of MODIS data (spatial resolution: 250m) (Figure 6 b)in 2006.

Brovey transformation fusion method was used.

$$DN_{fused} = DN_{pan} \times DN_{b1} / \left(DN_{b1} + DN_{b2} + DN_{b3}\right) \tag{4}$$

Where DN_{fused} means the DN of the resulting fused image produced from the input data in three MODIS multiple spectral bands ($DN_{b1,}$ DN_{b2}, DN_{b3}) multiplied by the high resolution Landsat ETM+ Pan band (DN_{pan}).

The building areas remained unchanged from 2000 to 2006 were in grey-pink. Meanwhile, the newly established buildings were in dark red color in the composed image (Figure 7) and could be easily identified.

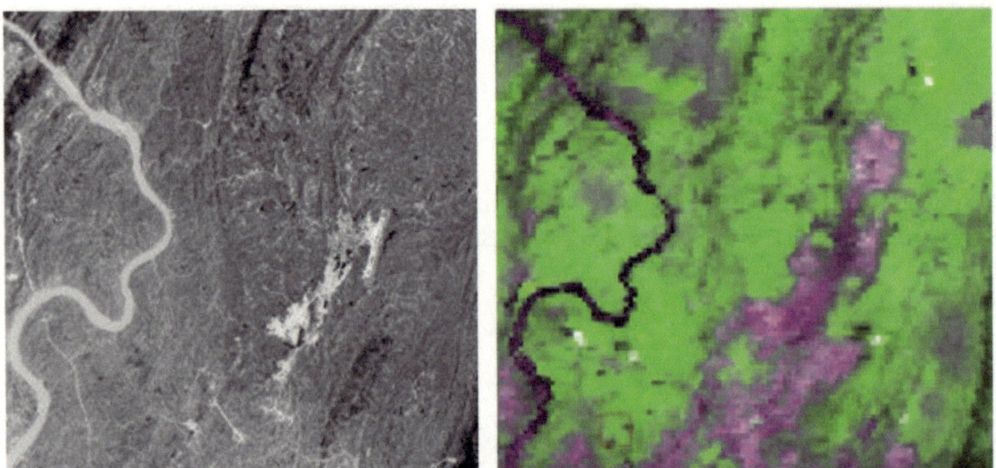

Figure 6. Satellite images of Chongqing City; a) ETM image, 2000 b) MODIS image, 2006

Figure 7. Fusion result of multiple sources images of Chongqing City

In recent years, object-oriented processing techniques are becoming more popular, compared to traditional pixel-based image analysis, object-oriented change information is necessary in decision support systems and uncertainty management strategies. An in-depth paper presented by Ruvimbo *et al.* introduced the concept and applications of object-oriented change detection for urban areas [43]. In general, due to the extensive statistical and derived information available with the object-oriented approach, a number of change images can be presented depending on research objectives. In land use and land cover analysis; this level of precision is valuable as analysis at the object level enables linkage with other GIS databases or derived socio-economic attributes.

4. Discussion and conclusions

Multi-sensor image fusion seeks to combine information from different images to obtain more inferences than can be derived from a single sensor. It is widely recognized as an efficient tool for improving overall performance in image based application. The chapter provides a state-of-art of multi-sensor image fusion in the field of remote sensing. Below are some emerging challenges and recommendations.

4.1. Improvements of fusion algorithms

Among the hundreds of variations of image fusion techniques, methods which had be widely used including IHS, PCA, Brovey transform, wavelet transform, and Artificial Neural Network (ANN). For methods like HIS, PCA and Brovey transform, which have lower complexity and faster processing time, the most significant problem is color distortion. Wavelet-based schemes perform better than those methods in terms of minimizing color distortion. The development of more sophisticated wavelet-based fusion algorithm (such as Ridgelet, Curvelet, and Contourlet transformation) could evidently improve performance result, but they often cause greater complexity in computation and parameters setting. Another challenge on existing fusion techniques will be the ability for processing hyper-spectral satellite sensor data. Artificial neural network seem to be one possible approach to handle the high dimension nature of hyper-spectral satellite sensor data.

4.2. From image fusion to multiple algorithm fusion

Each fusion method has its own set of advantages and limitations. The combination of several different fusion schemes has been approved to be the useful strategy which may achieve better quality of results. As a case in point, quite a few researchers have focused on incorporating the traditional IHS method into wavelet transforms, since the IHS fusion method performs well spatially while the wavelet methods perform well spectrally. However, selection and arrangement of those candidate fusion schemes are quite arbitrary and often depends upon the user's experience. Optimal combining strategy for different fusion algorithms, in another word, 'algorithm fusion' strategy, is thus urgent needed. Further investigations are necessary for the following aspects: 1) Design of a general framework for combination of different fusion approaches; 2) Development of new approaches which can combine aspects of pixel/feature/decision level image fusion; 3) Establishment of automatic quality assessment method for evaluation of fusion results.

4.3. Establishment of an automatic quality assessment scheme.

Automatic quality assessment is highly desirable to evaluate the possible benefits of fusion, to determine an optimal setting of parameters for a certain fusion scheme, as well as to compare results obtained with different algorithms. Mathematical methods were used to judge the quality of merged imagery in respect to their improvement of spatial resolution while preserving the spectral content of the data. Statistical indices, such as cross entropy, mean square error, signal-to-noise ratio, have been used for evaluation purpose. While recently a few image fusion quality measures have been proposed, analytical studies of these measures have been lacking. The work of Chen *et al.* focused on one popular mutual information-based quality measure and weighted averaging image fusion [44]. Zhao presented a new metric based on image phase congruency to assess the performance of the image fusion algorithm [45]. However, in general, no automatic solution has been achieved to consistently produce high quality fusion for different data sets. It is expected that the result of fusing data from multiple independent sensors will offer the potential for better performance than can be achieved by either sensor, and will reduce vulnerability to sensor specific countermeasures and deployment factors. We expect that future research will address new performance assessment criteria and automatic quality assessment methods [46].

Author details

Dong Jiang*, Dafang Zhuang and Yaohuan Huang

*Address all correspondence to: jiangd@igsnrr.ac.cn

State Key Lab of Resources and Environmental Information System, Institute of Geographical Sciences and Natural Resources Research, Chinese Academy of Sciences, Beijing, China

References

[1] Genderen, J. L. van, and Pohl, C. Image fusion: Issues, techniques and applications. Intelligent Image Fusion, Proceedings EARSeL Workshop, Strasbourg, France, 11 September 1994, edited by J. L. van Genderen and V. Cappellini (Enschede: ITC), 18-26.

[2] Guest editorial, Image fusion: Advances in the state of the art.(2007). *Information Fusion*.Vol.8, pp.114-118, ISSN 0018-9251

[3] Pohl, C.; Van Genderen, J.L. (1998). Multisensor image fusion in remote sensing: concepts, methods and applications. *Int. J. Remote Sens.Vol.* 19, pp.823-854,

[4] Hall, L.; Llinas, J. (1997).An introduction to multisensor data fusion. *Proc. IEEE*. Vol. 85, pp. 6-23, ISSN 0018-9219

[5] Simone, G.; Farina, A.; Morabito, F.C.; Serpico, S.B.; Bruzzone, L. (2002). Image fusion techniques for remote sensing applications. *Information Fusion* Vol.3, pp.3-15, ISSN 0018-9251

[6] Dasarathy, B.V. (2007). A special issue on image fusion: advances in the state of the art. *Information Fusion*. Vol.8, pp.113, ISSN 0018-9251

[7] Smith, M.I.; Heather, J.P. (2005). Review of image fusion technology in 2005. *In Proceedings of Defense and Security Symposium, Orlando, FL, USA, 2005.*

[8] Blum, R.S.; Liu, Z. (2006). Multi-Sensor Image Fusion and Its Applications; special series on Signal Processing and Communications; *CRC Press: Boca Raton, FL, USA,* 2006.

[9] Olivier TheÂpaut, Kidiyo Kpalma, Joseph Ronsin. (2000). Automatic registration of ERS and SPOT multisensory images in a data fusion context. *Forest Ecology and Management*. Vol.123, pp.93-100,

[10] Tamar Peli, Mon Young, Robert Knox, Kenneth K. Ellis and Frederick Bennett, Feature-level sensor fusion, Proc. SPIE 3719, 1999, 332

[11] Marcia L.S. Aguena, Nelson D.A. Mascarenhas.(2006). Multispectral image data fusion using POCS and super-resolution. *Computer Vision and Image Understanding* Vol. 102, pp.178-187,

[12] Ying Lei, Dong Jiang, and Xiaohuan Yang.(2007). Appllcation of image fusion in urban expanding detection. *Journal of Geomatics*, vol.32, No.3, pp.4-5, ISSN 1007-3817

[13] Ahmed F. Elaksher. (2008). Fusion of hyperspectral images and lidar-based dems for coastal mapping. *Optics and Lasers in Engineering* Vol.46, pp.493-498, ISSN 0143-8166

[14] Pouran, B.(2005). Comparison between four methods for data fusion of ETM+ multispectral and pan images. *Geo-spat. Inf. Sci.*Vol.8, pp.112-122, ISSN

[15] Adelson, C.H.; Bergen, J.R.(1984). Pyramid methods in image processing. *RCA Eng.* Vol.29, pp.33-41,

[16] Miao, Q.G.; Wang, B.S. (2007). Multi-sensor image fusion based on improved laplacian pyramid transform. *Acta Opti. Sin.* Vol.27, pp.1605-1610, ISSN 1424-8220

[17] Xiang, J.; Su, X. (2009). A pyramid transform of image denoising algorithm based on morphology. *Acta Photon. Sin.*Vol.38, pp.89-103, ISSN 1000-7032

[18] Mallat, S.G. (1989). A theory for multiresolution signal decomposition: the wavelet representation. *IEEE Trans. Pattern Anal. Mach. Intell.*Vol.11, pp.674-693, ISSN 0162-8828

[19] Ganzalo, P.; Jesus, M.A. (2004). Wavelet-based image fusion tutorial. *Pattern Recognit.* VOL.37, pp.1855-1872,

[20] Ma, H.; Jia, C.Y.; Liu, S. (2005).Multisource image fusion based on wavelet transform. *Int. J. Inf. Technol.* Vol. 11, pp 81-91,

[21] Candes, E.J.; Donoho, D.L.(2000). Curvelets-A Surprisingly Effective Nonadaptive Representation for Objects with Edges.Curves and Surfcaces; *Vanderbilt University Press: Nashville, TN, USA*, pp.105-120,

[22] Choi, M.; Kim, RY.; Nam, MR. Fusion of multi-spectral and panchromatic satellite images using the Curvelet transform. *IEEE Geosci. Remote Sens. Lett.* Vol.2, pp. 136-140, ISSN 0196-2892

[23] Donoho, M.N.; Vetterli, M. (2002).Contourlets; *Academic Press: New York, NY, USA*, ISSN 0890-5401

[24] Dong. J.; Yang, X.; Clinton, N.; Wang, N. (2004).An artificial neural network model for estimating crop yields using remotely sensed information. *Int. J. Remote Sens.* Vol. 25, pp. 1723-1732, ISSN 0143-1161

[25] Shutao, L.; Kwok, J.T.; Yaonan W.(2002). Multifocus image fusion using artificial neural networks. *Pattern Recognit. Lett.* Vol. 23, pp. 985-997., ISSN 0167-8655

[26] Thomas, F.; Grzegorz, G. (1995).Optimal fusion of TV and infrared images using artificial neural networks. *In Proceedings of Applications and Science of Artificial Neural Networks, Orlando, FL, USA, April 21, 1995*;Vol. 2492, pp.919-925,

[27] Huang, W.; Jing, Z.(2007). Multi-focus image fusion using pulse coupled neural network. *Pattern Recognit. Lett.* Vol. 28, pp.1123-1132,, ISSN 0167-8655

[28] Wu, Y.; Yang, W. (2003).Image fusion based on wavelet decomposition and evolutionary strategy. *Acta Opt. Sin.* Vol. 23, pp. 671-676,

[29] Sun, Z.Z.; Fu, K.; Wu, Y.R. (2003).The high-resolution SAR image terrain classification algorithm based on mixed double hint layers RBFN model. *Acta Electron. Sin. Vol.*, 31, pp. 2040-2044,

[30] Zhang, H.; Sun, X.N.; Zhao, L.; Liu, L. (2008).Image fusion algorithm using RBF neural networks. *Lect. Notes Comput. Sci.* Vol. 9, pp. 417-424,

[31] Gail, A.; Siegfried, M.; Ogas, J.(2005). Self-organizing information fusion and hierarchical knowledge discovery- a new framework using ARTMAP neural networks. *Neural Netw.* Vol. 18, pp.287-295,

[32] Wang, R.; Bu, F.L.; Jin, H.; Li, L.H.(2007). A feature-level image fusion algorithm based on neural networks. *Bioinf. Biomed. Eng.* Vol. 7, pp. 821-824,

[33] Huadong Wu;Mel Siegel; Rainer Stiefelhagen;Jie Yang.(2002).Sensor Fusion Using Dempster-Shafer Theory, *IEEE Instrumentation and Measurement Technology Conference Anchorage, AK, USA, 21-23 May 2002,*

[34] S. Le Hégarat-Mascle, D. Richard, C. (2003).Ottlé, Multi-scale data fusion using Dempster-Shafer evidence theory, Integrated Computer-Aided Engineering, Vol.10, No.1, pp.9-22, ISSN: 1875-8835

[35] H. Borotschnig, L. Paletta, M. Prantl, and A. Pinz, Graz. (1999).A Comparison of Probabilistic, Possibilistic and Evidence Theoretic Fusion Schemes for Active Object Recognition. *Computing*. Vol.62, pp. 293–319,

[36] Jin, X.Y.; Davis, C.H. (2005).An integrated system for automatic road mapping from high-resolution multi-spectral satellite imagery by information fusion. *Inf. Fusion Vol.* 6, pp.257-273, ISSN 0018-9251

[37] Garzelli, A.; Nencini, F. (2007).Panchromatic sharpening of remote sensing images using a multiscale Kalman filter. *Pattern Recognit.*Vol. 40, pp. 3568-3577, ISSN: 0167-8655

[38] Wu, Y.; Yang, W.(2003). Image fusion based on wavelet decomposition and evolutionary strategy. *Acta Opt. Sin.*Vol. 23, pp.671-676, ISSN 0253-2239

[39] Sarkar, A.; Banerjee, A.; Banerjee, N.; Brahma, S.; Kartikeyan, B.; Chakraborty, M.; Majumder, K.L.(2005). Landcover classification in MRF context using Dempster-Shafer fusion for multisensor imagery. IEEE Trans. *Image Processing*, Vol.14, pp. 634-645, ISSN : 1057-7149

[40] Liu, C.P.; Ma, X.H.; Cui, Z.M.(2007). Multi-source remote sensing image fusion classification based on DS evidence theory. *In Proceedings of Conference on Remote Sensing and GIS Data Processing and Applications; and Innovative Multispectral Technology and Applications, Wuhan, China, November 15–17, 2007;* Vol. 6790, part 2.

[41] Rottensteiner, F.; Trinder, J.; Clode, S.; Kubik, K.; Lovell, B.(2004).Building detection by Dempster-Shafer fusion of LIDAR data and multispectral aerial imagery. *In Proceedings of the 17th International Conference on Pattern Recognition, Cambridge, UK, August 23–26, 2004;* Vol. 2, pp. 339-342, ISSN: 1001-0920

[42] Madhavan, B.B.; Sasagawa, T.; Tachibana, K.; Mishra, K.(2005). A decision level fusion of ADS-40, TABI and AISA data. *Nippon Shashin Sokuryo Gakkai Gakujutsu Koenkai Happyo Ronbunshu*, Vol.2005, 163-166

[43] Ruvimbo, G.;Philippe, D.; Morgan, D.(2009). Object-oriented change detection for the city of Harare, Zimbabwe. *Exp. Syst. Appl.*Vol. 36, pp.571-588, ISSN 0013-8703

[44] Chen, Y.; Xue, Z.Y.; Blum, R.S. (2008).Theoretical analysis of an information-based quality measure for image fusion. *Information Fusion*, Vol. 9, pp. 161-175, ISSN 0018-9251

[45] Zhao, J.Y.; Laganiere, R.; Liu, Z.(2006). Image fusion algorithm assessment based on feature measurement. In Proceedings of the 1st International Conference on Innovative Computing, Information and Control, Beijing, China, August 30 – September 1, Vol. 2, pp. 701-704,

[46] Dong Jiang;Dafang Zhuang, ; Yaohuan Huang; Jingying Fu.(2009). Advances in multi-sensor data fusion: algorithms and applications. *Sensors*, Vol.9, No.10, pp. 7771-7784, ISSN 1424-8220

Chapter 2

A Multi-Features Fusion of Multi-Temporal Hyperspectral Images Using a Cooperative GDD/SVM Method

Selim Hemissi and Imed Riadh Farah

Additional information is available at the end of the chapter

http://dx.doi.org/10.5772/56949

1. Introduction

Considering the emergence of hyperspectral sensors, feature fusion has been more and more important for images classification, indexing and retrieval. In this chapter, a cooperative fusion method GDD/SVM (Generalized Dirichlet Distribution/Support Vector Machines), which involves heterogeneous features, is proposed for multi-temporal hyperspectral images classification. It differentiates, from most of the previous approaches, by incorporating the potentials of generative models into a discriminative classifier. Therefore, the multi-features, including the 3D spectral features and textural features, can be integrated with an efficient way into a unified robust framework. The experimental results on a series of Hyperion images show that the precision is 92.64% and the recall is 91.87%. The experiments on AVIRIS dataset also confirm the improved performance and show that this cooperative fusion approach has consistence over different testing datasets.

2. Problem statement

The semantic categorization of remote-sensing images requires analysis of many features of the images such as texture, spectral profiles, etc. Current feature fusion approaches commonly concatenate different features. It gives, generally good results and several approaches have been proposed using this schema. However, most of them have various conditional constraints, such as noise and imperfection, which might retain the use of such systems under degraded performance. However, how to fuse heterogeneous features in a flexible way is still an open research question.

Similarly, in the area of Supervised Machine Learning (SML), diversity with respect to the errors committed by component classifiers has received much attention. Generative and discriminative approaches are two distinct schools of probabilistic machine learning. It has shown that discriminative approaches such as SVM [1] outperform model based approaches due to their flexibility in decision boundaries estimation. Conversely, since that discriminative methods are concerned with boundaries, all the classes need to be estimated conjointly [2]. Complementary, one of the interesting characteristics, that generative models have over discriminative ones, is that they are learnt independently for each class. Moreover, following their modeling power, generative models are able to deal with missing data. An ideal fusion method should combine these two approaches in order to improve the classification accuracy.

3. Theoretical background

3.1. Generalized dirichlet distribution

Priors based on Dirichlet location-scale mixture of normals are widely used to model densities as mixtures of normal kernels. A random density f arising from such a prior can be expressed as

$$f(y) = (\phi * P)(y) = \int \frac{1}{\sigma}\phi\left(\frac{y-\theta}{\sigma}\right) dP(\theta,\sigma), \tag{1}$$

where $\phi(\cdot)$ is the standard normal density and the mixing distribution P follows a Dirichlet process.

[3] initiated a theoretical study of these priors for the problem of density estimation. They showed that if a density f_0 satisfies certain conditions, then a Dirichlet location mixture of normals achieves posterior consistency at f_0. Their conditions can be best summarized as f_0 having a moment generating function on an open interval containing $[-1,1]$. Ghosal and van der Vaart (2001) extended these results to rate calculations for the more general Dirichlet location-scale mixture prior. However, they restricted the scale parameter σ to a compact interval $[\underline{\sigma},\overline{\sigma}] \subset (0,\infty)$.

3.1.1. *Preliminaries*

To make this chapter relatively self-contained, we recall the definitions of posterior consistency in the context of density estimation and regression. These definitions formalize the concept that in order to achieve consistency, the posterior should concentrate on arbitrarily small neighborhoods of the true model when more observations are made available.

Posterior consistency for density estimation: Suppose $X_1, X_2, \cdots$ are independent and identically distributed according to an unknown density f_0. We take the parameter space as $\mathcal{F}$ - a set of probability densities on the space of the observations and consider a prior distribution Π on $\mathcal{F}$. Then the posterior distribution $\Pi(\cdot|X_1,\cdots,X_n)$ given a sample $X_1,\cdots,X_n$ is obtained as,

$$\Pi(A|X_1,\cdots,X_n) = \frac{\int_A \prod_{i=1}^n f(X_i)d\Pi(f)}{\int_{\mathcal{F}} \prod_{i=1}^n f(X_i)d\Pi(f)}.$$

We say that the posterior achieves weak (or strong) posterior consistency at f_0 if for any weak (or L_1) neighborhood U of f_0, $\Pi(U|X_1,X_2,\cdots,X_n) \to 1$ almost surely as $n \to \infty$.

Posterior consistency for regression: Suppose one observes $Y_1,Y_2,\cdots$ from the model $Y_i = \alpha_0 + \beta_0 x_i + \epsilon_i$, where x_i's are known non-random covariate values and ϵ_i's are independent and identically distributed with an unknown symmetric density f_0. The regression coefficients α_0,β_0 are also unknown. Here, it is appropriate to consider the parameter space as $\Theta = \mathcal{F}^* \times \mathbb{R} \times \mathbb{R}$, where $\mathcal{F}^*$ is a set of symmetric probability densities on $\mathbb{R}$ with a prior Π on Θ. The posterior distribution $\Pi(\cdot|Y_!,\cdots,Y_n)$ is then computed as,

$$\Pi(A|Y_1,\cdots,Y_n) = \frac{\int_A \prod_{i=1}^n f(Y_i-\alpha-\beta x_i)d\Pi(f,\alpha,\beta)}{\int_\times \prod_{i=1}^n f(Y_i-\alpha-\beta x_i)d\Pi(f,\alpha,\beta)}.$$

We say that the posterior achieves weak consistency at (f_0,α_0,β_0) if for any weak neighborhood U of f_0 and any $\delta > 0$,

$$\Pi((f,\alpha,\beta) : f \in U, |\alpha-\alpha_0| < \delta, |\beta-\beta_0| < \delta|Y_1,Y_2,\cdots,Y_n) \to 1$$

almost surely as $n \to \infty$.

3.1.2. Density estimation: weak consistency

We start with weak posterior consistency for the problem of density estimation. Our main tool is the following theorem due to Schwartz (1965).

A prior Π achieves weak posterior consistency at a density f_0, if

$$\forall\epsilon > 0,\ \Pi\left(f \in \mathcal{F} : \int f_0(x)\log\frac{f_0(x)}{f(x)}dx < \epsilon\right) > 0 \tag{2}$$

We would use the notation $f_0 \in KL(\Pi)$ to indicate that a density f_0 satisfies (2).

General Mixture Priors First consider the case when the mixing distribution P in (1) follows some general distribution $\tilde{\Pi}$, not necessarily a Dirichlet process. It is *reasonable* to assume that the weak support of $\tilde{\Pi}$ contains all probability measures on $\mathbb{R} \times \mathbb{R}^+$ that are compactly supported. The next lemma reveals the implication of this property.

Consider an $f_0 \in \mathcal{F}$ such that $\int x^2 f_0(x)dx < \infty$. Suppose $\tilde{f} = \phi * \tilde{P}$ is such that $\tilde{P}((-a,a) \times (\underline{\sigma},\overline{\sigma})) = 1$ for some $a > 0, 0 < \underline{\sigma} < \overline{\sigma}$. Then for any $\epsilon > 0$, there exists a weak neighborhood W of $\tilde{P}$ such that for any $f = \phi * P$ with $P \in W$,

$$\int f_0(x)\log\frac{\tilde{f}(x)}{f(x)}dx < \epsilon \tag{3}$$

The proof of this lemma is similar to the proof of Theorem 3 of Ghosal *et al.* (1999) and we present it in the appendix. Here we state and prove the main result.

Let $f_0(x)$ be a continuous density on $\mathbb{R}$ satisfying:

1. f_0 is nowhere zero and bounded above by $M < \infty$.
2. $\left|\int_{\mathbb{R}} f_0(x) \log f_0(x) dx\right| < \infty$.
3. $\int_{\mathbb{R}} f_0(x) \log \frac{f_0(x)}{\psi_1(x)} dx < \infty$ where $\psi_1(x) = \inf_{t \in [x-1, x+1]} f_0(t)$.
4. $\exists \eta > 0$ such that $\int_{\mathbb{R}} |x|^{2(1+\eta)} f_0(x) dx < \infty$.

Then, $f_0 \in KL(\Pi)$.

Assumption 4 provides the important moment condition on f_0. Assumption 2 is satisfied by most of the common densities and assumption 3 can be viewed as a regularity conditions. The interval $[x-1, x+1]$ that appears in assumption 3 can be replaced by $[x-a, x+a]$ for any $a > 0$.

Proof. **of Theorem 3.1.2** Note that,

$$\int f_0(x) \log \frac{f_0(x)}{f(x)} dx = \int f_0(x) \log \frac{f_0(x)}{\tilde{f}(x)} dx + \int f_0(x) \log \frac{\tilde{f}(x)}{f(x)} dx. \tag{4}$$

Therefore, the result would follow if for any $\epsilon > 0$, we can find an $\tilde{f}$ which makes $\int f_0 \log \frac{f_0}{\tilde{f}} dx < \epsilon/2$ and also satisfies the condition of Lemma 3.1.2. Next we show how to construct such an $\tilde{f}$.

Consider the densities $f_n = \phi * P_n$, $n \geq 1$, with P_n's constructed as,

$$dP_n(\theta, \sigma) = t_n I_{(\theta \in [-n,n])} f_0(\theta) \delta_{\sigma_n}(\sigma) \tag{5}$$

where $\sigma_n = n^{-\eta}$, $t_n = (\int_{-n}^{n} f_0(y) dy)^{-1}$, I_A is the indicator function of a set A and δ_x is the point mass at a point x. Note that f_n can be simply written as,

$$f_n(x) = t_n \int_{-n}^{n} \frac{1}{\sigma_n} \phi\left(\frac{x-\theta}{\sigma_n}\right) f_0(\theta) d\theta. \tag{6}$$

Find a positive constant ξ such that $\int_{-\xi}^{\xi} \phi(t) dt > 1 - \epsilon$. Now fix an $x \in \mathbb{R}$. For sufficiently large n such that $[x - \xi\sigma_n, x + \xi\sigma_n] \subset [-n, n]$, one obtains,

$$\inf_{y \in (x-\xi\sigma_n, x+\xi\sigma_n)} f_0(y)(1-\epsilon) < \frac{f_n(x)}{t_n} < \sup_{y \in (x-\xi\sigma_n, x+\xi\sigma_n)} f_0(y) + M\epsilon \tag{7}$$

Since $t_n \to 1$ and $\sigma_n \to 0$, (7) would imply that $f_n(x) \to f_0(x)$ as $n \to \infty$ by continuity of f_0. Therefore one can conclude,

$$\log \frac{f_0(x)}{f_n(x)} \to 0 \text{ for all } x \in \mathbb{R} \tag{8}$$

Since t_n is a decreasing sequence and $f_0(\theta) < M$ for all $\theta \in \mathbb{R}$, one can readily see that for all $n \geq 1$ and all $x \in \mathbb{R}$,

$$f_n(x) = t_n \int_{-n}^{n} \frac{1}{\sigma_n} \phi\left(\frac{x-\theta}{\sigma_n}\right) f_0(\theta) d\theta \leq M t_n \leq M t_1. \tag{9}$$

Now, fix an $x \in \mathbb{R}$. Since, $|x - \theta| \leq |x| + n$ for all $\theta \in [-n, n]$ and $t_n \geq 1$, it follows that for all $n \leq |x|$,

$$f_n(x) \geq \frac{1}{\sigma_n} \phi\left(\frac{|x|+n}{\sigma_n}\right) = n^{\eta} \phi(n^{\eta}(|x|+n)) \geq |x|^{\eta} \phi(2|x|^{1+\eta}). \tag{10}$$

The last inequality follows from the fact that $\tau^{\eta}\phi(\tau^{\eta}(|x|+\tau))$ is decreasing in τ for $\tau \geq 1$.

Let $\psi_n(x) = \inf_{t \in [x-\sigma_n, x+\sigma_n]} f_0(t)$. It may be noted that the function $\psi_1(x)$ of assumption 3 is consistent with this definition. Let $A_n = [-n, n] \cap [x - \sigma_n, x + \sigma_n]$ and $c = \int_0^1 \phi(t) dt < 1$. Observe that for all $n > |x|$,

$$f_n(x) \geq t_n \int_{A_n} \frac{1}{\sigma_n} \phi\left(\frac{x-\theta}{\sigma_n}\right) f_0(\theta) d\theta \geq t_n \psi_n(x) \int_{A_n} \frac{1}{\sigma_n} \phi\left(\frac{x-\theta}{\sigma_n}\right) d\theta \tag{11}$$

Since $t_n \geq 1$, $\psi_n(x) \geq \psi_1(x)$ and $\int_{A_n} \frac{1}{\sigma_n}\phi(\frac{x-\theta}{\sigma_n}) d\theta \geq \int_0^1 \phi(t) dt = c$ for all $n \geq 1$ and all $x \in \mathbb{R}$ it follows from (11) that $f_n(x) \geq c\psi_1(x)$ for all $n > |x|$.. Therefore,

$$f_n(x) \geq \begin{cases} c\psi_1(x) & |x| < 1 \\ \min(|x|^{\eta}\phi(2|x|^{1+\eta}), c\psi_1(x)) & |x| \geq 1 \end{cases} \tag{12}$$

A little algebraic manipulation with (9) and (12) obtains, $\forall n \geq 1$,

$$\left|\log \frac{f_0(x)}{f_n(x)}\right| \leq \log \frac{M t_1}{f_0(x)} + \log \frac{f_0(x)}{c\psi_1(x)} + I_{\{|x|>1\}} \log \frac{f_0(x)}{|x|^{\eta}\phi(2|x|^{1+\eta})} \tag{13}$$

From the assumptions of Theorem 3.2, it can be easily verified that the function on the right hand side of the above display is f_0 integrable. Therefore an application of DCT on (8) implies that,

$$\lim_{n \to \infty} \int f_0(x) \log \frac{f_0(x)}{f_n(x)} dx = 0. \tag{14}$$

Therefore we can simply choose $\tilde{f} = f_{n_0}$ for some large enough n_0.

□

3.2. Dirichlet mixture of normals

Next we consider $\tilde{\Pi} = Dir(\alpha G_0)$, a Dirichlet process with parameter αG_0. Here α is a positive constant and G_0 is a probability measure on $\mathbb{R} \times \mathbb{R}^+$.

Suppose $f_0 \in \mathcal{F}$ satisfies the following property: For any $0 < \tau < 1, \epsilon > 0$, there exist a set $\mathcal{A}$ and a positive number x_0 such that $\tilde{\Pi}(\mathcal{A}) > 1 - \tau$ and for any $f = \phi * P$ with $P \in \mathcal{A}$,

$$\int_{|x|>x_0} f_0(x) \log \frac{f_0(x)}{f(x)} dx < \epsilon. \tag{15}$$

Then, $f_0 \in KL(\Pi)$.

Note that the moment condition of Theorem 3.1.2 is substantially reduced.

Let f_0 be a density on $\mathbb{R}$ satisfying

1. $\int f_0(x) \log f_0(x) dx < \infty$.
2. $\exists\, \eta \in (0,1)$ such that $\int |x|^\eta f_0(x) dx < \infty$.

Further assume that there exist $\sigma_0 > 0$, $0 < \beta < \eta$, $\gamma > \beta$ and $b_1, b_2 > 0$ such that for large $x > 0$

3. $\max\left(G_0\left(\left[x - \sigma_0 x^{\frac{\eta}{2}}, \infty\right) \times [\sigma_0, \infty)\right), G_0\left([0,\infty) \times (x^{1-\frac{\eta}{2}}, \infty)\right)\right) \geq b_1 x^{-\beta}$
4. $G_0\left((-\infty, x) \times (0, e^{|x|^\eta - \frac{1}{2}})\right) > 1 - b_2 |x|^{-\gamma}$.

and for large $x < 0$,

3′. $\max\left(G_0\left(\left(-\infty, x + \sigma_0 |x|^{\frac{\eta}{2}}\right] \times [\sigma_0, \infty)\right), G_0\left((-\infty, 0] \times (|x|^{1-\frac{\eta}{2}}, \infty)\right)\right) \geq b_1 |x|^{-\beta}$

4.′ $G_0\left((x, \infty) \times (0, e^{|x|^\eta - \frac{1}{2}})\right) > 1 - b_2 |x|^{-\gamma}$.

then $f_0 \in KL(\Pi)$. Other than the important moment condition on f_0 this theorem also requires some regularity in the tail of the base measure G_0. For example, assumption *3,3′* requires the tail of G_0 not to decay faster than a polynomial rate for the scale parameter σ. This condition seems very reasonable since the Cauchy density itself can be written as a scale mixture of normals with the mixing density having a polynomial decay towards infinity.

A standard choice for G_0 is the conjugate normal-inverse gamma distribution (see Escobar and West 1995), under which, $\theta|\sigma \sim N(0, \xi\sigma^2)$ and $\sigma^{-2} \sim Gamma(r, \lambda)$, for some $\xi, r, \lambda > 0$. For such a G_0 with $r \in (1/2, 1)$, one can show that the conditions of Theorem 3.2 hold true with $\eta \in (2r/(1+r), 1)$, $\beta = r(2-\eta)$ and $\gamma = 2r$. For example, the conditions in *Assumptions 3, 3′* are satisfied since,

$$G_0\left([0,\infty) \times (x^{1-\frac{\eta}{2}}, \infty)\right) = \frac{1}{2} \Pr(\sigma^{-2} \leq x^{-(2-\eta)}) = c \int_0^{x^{-(2-\eta)}} v^{r-1} e^{-\lambda v} dv \leq c' x^{-r(2-\eta)},$$

for some positive constants c, c'. To see that the conditions of *Assumptions 4, 4'* also hold, note that,

$$1 - G_0\left((-\infty, x) \times (0, e^{|x|^\eta - \frac{1}{2}})\right) \le \Pr(\theta > x) + \Pr(\sigma^{-2} < e^{-2|x|^\eta + 1}).$$

An argument similar to the one provided above shows that the second term, namely, $\Pr(\sigma^{-2} < e^{-2|x|^\eta+1})$ is bounded by a constant times $e^{-2r|x|^\eta + r}$. Therefore, this term can be made smaller than $c|x|^{-\gamma}$ for a suitable constant c. Now, using the inequality $1 - \Phi(X) \le (1/x)\phi(x)$, where $\Phi(\cdot)$ and $\phi(\cdot)$ are the standard normal distribution and density functions, we obtain

$$\Pr(\theta > x) \le \frac{c}{x}\int_0^\infty v^{r-1/2-1} e^{-(\frac{x^2}{2\xi}+\lambda)v} dv = \frac{c'}{x(\frac{x^2}{2\xi}+\lambda)^{r-1/2}} \le \frac{c''}{x^{2r}}$$

for some positive constants c, c', c''. The desired inequality follows from these two bounds. Therefore, such a choice of G_0 would lead to posterior consistency, for example, when f_0 is a Cauchy density.

Proof. **of Theorem 3.2** We simply need show that such an f_0 satisfies the condition of Lemma 3.2. Let $w(x) = \exp(-x^\eta),\ x \ge 0$. Define a class of subsets of $\mathbb{R} \times \mathbb{R}^+$ indexed by $x \in \mathbb{R}$, as follows:

$$K_x = \left\{(\theta, \sigma) \in \mathbb{R} \times \mathbb{R}^+ : \frac{1}{\sigma}\phi\left(\frac{x-\theta}{\sigma}\right) \ge \frac{1}{\sqrt{2\pi}} w(|x|)\right\} \tag{16}$$

These sets are of particular interest, since for $f = \phi * P$,

$$\begin{aligned}\int_{|x|>x_0} f_0(x)\log\frac{f_0(x)}{f(x)}dx &\le \int_{|x|>x_0} f_0(x)\log\frac{f_0(x)}{\int_{K_x}\frac{1}{\sigma}\phi\left(\frac{x-\theta}{\sigma}\right)dP(\theta,\sigma)}dx \\ &\le \int_{|x|>x_0} f_0(x)\log\frac{f_0(x)}{\frac{1}{\sqrt{2\pi}}w(|x|)P(K_x)}dx \\ &\le \int_{|x|>x_0} f_0(x)\left\{\log f_0(x) + |x|^\eta + \log\frac{\sqrt{2\pi}}{P(K_x)}\right\}dx. \end{aligned} \tag{17}$$

By the assumptions of the Theorem, this quantity can be made arbitrarily small for a suitably large x_0 if we can show that $P(K_x) > c_1 \exp(-c_2|x|^\eta)$ for all $|x| > x_0$ for some fixed constants $c_1, c_2 > 0$. Therefore it suffices to prove that, For any $\tau > 0$ there exists an $x_0 > 0$ and a set $\mathcal{A}$ with $\tilde{\Pi}(\mathcal{A}) > 1 - \tau$ such that $P \in \mathcal{A} \Rightarrow P(K_x) \ge (1/2)\exp(-2|x|^\eta/b_1)$ for all $|x| > x_0$.

The proof of this Lemma is fairly technical. It makes an extensive use of the tail behavior of a random probability P arising from a Dirichlet process. For clarity of reading, we present details of the proof in the Appendix.

□

4. Density estimation: strong consistency

We establish L_1-consistency of a Dirichlet location-scale mixture of normal prior Π by verifying the conditions of Theorem 8 of Ghosal *et al.* (1999). This theorem is reproduced below.

Let Π be a prior on $\mathcal{F}$ such that $f_0 \in KL(\Pi)$. If there is a $\delta < \epsilon/4, c_1, c_2 > 0, \beta < \epsilon^2/8$ and $\mathcal{F}_n \subseteq \mathcal{F}$ such that for all n large,

1. $\Pi(\mathcal{F}_n^c) < c_1 e^{-nc_2}$,
2. $J(\delta, \mathcal{F}_n) < n\beta$,

then Π achieves strong posterior consistency at f_0.

Here $J(\delta, \mathcal{G})$ denotes logarithm of the covering number of $\mathcal{G}$ by L_1 balls of radii δ.

We first show how to calculate $J(\delta, \mathcal{G})$ for certain type of sets $\mathcal{G}$. For some $a > 0,\ u > l > 0$ define

$$\mathcal{F}_{a,l,u} = \{f = \phi * P : P\left((-a,a] \times (l,u]\right) = 1\} \tag{18}$$

Then,

$$J(2\kappa, \mathcal{F}_{a,l,u}) \leq b_0 \left(b_1 \frac{a}{l} + b_2 \log \frac{u}{l} + 1\right). \tag{19}$$

where b_0, b_1 and b_2 depend upon κ but not on a, l or u.

Proof. Let $\phi_{\theta,\sigma}$ denote the normal density with mean θ and standard deviation σ. For $\sigma_2 > \sigma_1 > \sigma_2/2$, it can be shown that,

$$\begin{aligned} \left\|\phi_{\theta_1,\sigma_1} - \phi_{\theta_2,\sigma_2}\right\| &\leq \left\|\phi_{\theta_1,\sigma_2} - \phi_{\theta_2,\sigma_2}\right\| + \left\|\phi_{\theta_2,\sigma_1} - \phi_{\theta_2,\sigma_2}\right\| \\ &\leq \sqrt{\frac{2}{\pi}} \frac{|\theta_2 - \theta_1|}{\sigma_2} + 3\frac{\sigma_2 - \sigma_1}{\sigma_1}. \end{aligned} \tag{20}$$

Let $\zeta = \min(\kappa/6, 1)$. Define $\sigma_m = l(1+\zeta)^m,\ m \geq 0$. Let M be the smallest integer such that $\sigma_M = l(1+\zeta)^M \geq u$. This implies $M \leq (1+\zeta)^{-1} \log(u/l) + 1$. For $1 \leq j \leq M$, let $N_j = \left\lceil \sqrt{\frac{32}{\pi}} a/(\kappa\sigma_{j-1}) \right\rceil$. For $1 \leq i \leq N_j;\ 1 \leq j \leq M$, define

$$E_{ij} = \left(-a + \frac{2a(i-1)}{N_j},\ -a + \frac{2ai}{N_j}\right] \times (\sigma_{j-1}, \sigma_j]. \tag{21}$$

Then, $(\theta, \sigma),\ (\theta', \sigma') \in E_{ij} \Rightarrow \left\|\phi_{\theta,\sigma} - \phi_{\theta',\sigma'}\right\| < \kappa$. Take $N = \sum_{j=1}^{M} N_j$ and let

$$\mathcal{P}_N = \left\{(P_{11}, \cdots, P_{N_1 1}, \cdots, P_{1M}, \cdots, P_{N_M M}) : P_{ij} \geq 0, \sum_{ij} P_{ij} = 1\right\} \tag{22}$$

be the N dimensional probability simplex and $\mathcal{P}_N^*$ be a κ-net in $\mathcal{P}_N$. Let τ_j's be as before and $\theta_{ij} = -a + 2a(i - 1/2)/N_j$, $1 \le i \le N_j$, $1 \le j \le M$. So $(\theta_{ij}, \sigma_j) \in E_{ij}\ \forall i, j$. It can be shown by following an argument similar to the one presented in the proof of Lemma 1 of Ghosal *et al.* (1999) that ,

$$\mathcal{F} = \left\{ \sum_{j=1}^{M} \sum_{i=1}^{N_j} P_{ij}^* \phi_{\theta_{ij},\sigma_j} : P^* \in \mathcal{P}_N^* \right\} \tag{23}$$

is a 2κ-net in $\mathcal{F}_{a,l,u}$ and consequently, $J(2\kappa, \mathcal{F}_{a,l,u}) \le J(\kappa, \mathcal{P}_N) \le N\left(1 + \log \frac{1+\kappa}{\kappa}\right)$. But,

$$\begin{aligned} N &\le \sum_{j=1}^{M} \left(\sqrt{\frac{32}{\pi}} \frac{a}{\sigma_{j-1}\kappa} + 1 \right) = \sqrt{\frac{32}{\pi}} \frac{a}{l\kappa} \sum_{j=0}^{M-1} (1+\zeta)^{-j} + M \\ &\le \sqrt{\frac{32}{\pi}} \frac{a}{l} \frac{1+\zeta}{\kappa\zeta} + \frac{1}{1+\zeta} \log \frac{u}{l} + 1 \\ &= b_1 \frac{a}{l} + b_2 \log \frac{u}{l} + 1 \end{aligned} \tag{24}$$

From this the result follows with $b_0 = 1 + \log \frac{1+\kappa}{\kappa}$. □

Let $\mathcal{F}_{a,l,u}^{\kappa} = \{ f = \phi * P : P((-a,a] \times (l,u]) \ge 1 - \kappa \}$. Then $J(3\kappa, \mathcal{F}_{a,l,u}^{\kappa}) \le J(\kappa, \mathcal{F}_{a,l,u})$.

Proof. Let $f = \phi * P \in \mathcal{F}_{a,l,u}^{\kappa}$. Consider the probability measure defined by $P^*(A) = P(A \cap (-a,a] \times (l,u])/P((-a,a] \times (l,u])$. Then the density $f^* = \phi * P^*$ clearly belongs to $\mathcal{F}_{a,l,u}$ and further satisfies $\|f - f^*\| < 2\kappa$. This proves the lemma.

□

Suppose for each $\kappa > 0, \beta > 0$, there exist sequences of positive numbers $a_n, u_n \uparrow \infty, l_n \downarrow 0$ with $l_n < u_n$ and constant β_0, all depending on κ and β such that

1. $\tilde{\Pi}\left(\{P : P((-a_n, a_n] \times (l_n, u_n]) < 1 - \kappa\}\right) < e^{-n\beta_0}$,
2. $a_n/l_n < n\beta$, $\log(u_n/l_n) < n\beta$.

then $f_0 \in KL(\Pi)$ implies that Π achieves strong posterior consistency at f_0.

Proof. Take $\mathcal{F}_n = \mathcal{F}_{a_n,l_n,u_n}^{\kappa}$. Then the conditions of Theorem 4 are easily verified using Lemma 4 for a suitable choice of $\kappa > 0$. □

If $\tilde{\Pi} = Dir(\alpha G_0)$, verification of conditions 1 and 2 becomes particularly simple. For example, if G_0 is a product of a normal on θ and an inverse gamma on σ^2, then the conditions of theorem 4 are satisfied if $a_n = O(\sqrt{n}), l_n = O(1/\sqrt{n})$ and $u_n = O(e^n)$.

4.1. Support vector machines

We give, in this section, a very brief presentation of Support Vector Machines (SVMs) that is needed for the definition of their functional versions. We refer the reader to e.g. [4] for a more comprehensive presentation. As stated in section **??**, $\mathcal{X}$ denotes an arbitrary Hilbert space. Our presentation of SVM departs from the standard introduction because it assumes that the observations belong to $\mathcal{X}$ rather than to a d. This will make clear that the definition of SVM on arbitrary Hilbert spaces is not the difficult part in the construction of functional SVM. We will discuss problems related to the functional nature of the data in section 4.1.5.

Our goal is to classify data into two predefined classes. We assume given a learning set, i.e. N examples $(x_1, y_1), \ldots, (x_N, y_N)$ which are i.i.d. realizations of the random variable pair (X, Y) where X has values in $\mathcal{X}$ and Y in $\{-1, 1\}$, i.e. Y is the class label for X which is the observation.

4.1.1. Hard margin SVM

The principle of SVM is to perform an affine discrimination of the observations with maximal margin, that is to find an element $w \in \mathcal{X}$ with a minimum norm and a real value b, such that $y_i(\langle w, x_i \rangle + b) \geq 1$ for all i. To do so, we have to solve the following quadratic programming problem:

$$(P_0)\ \min_{w,b} \langle w, w \rangle, \text{ subject to } y_i(\langle w, x_i \rangle + b) \geq 1,\ 1 \leq i \leq N.$$

The classification rule associated to (w, b) is simply $(x) = \text{sign}(\langle w, x \rangle + b)$. In this situation (called hard margin SVM), we request the rule to have zero error on the learning set.

4.1.2. Soft margin SVM

In practice, the solution provided by problem (P_0) is not very satisfactory. Firstly, perfectly linearly separable problems are quite rare, partly because non linear problems are frequent, but also because noise can turn a linearly separable problem into a non separable one. Secondly, choosing a classifier with maximal margin does not prevent overfitting, especially in very high dimensional spaces (see e.g. [5] for a discussion about this point).

A first step to solve this problem is to allow some classification errors on the learning set. This is done by replacing (P_0) by its soft margin version, i.e., by the problem:

$$\begin{aligned} (P_C)\ \min_{w,b,\xi} \langle w, w \rangle + C \textstyle\sum_{i=1}^{N} \xi_i, \\ \text{subject to } y_i(\langle w, x_i \rangle + b) \geq 1 - \xi_i,\ 1 \leq i \leq N, \\ \xi_i \geq 0,\ 1 \leq i \leq N. \end{aligned}$$

Classification errors are allowed thanks to the slack variables ξ_i. The C parameter acts as an inverse regularization parameter. When C is small, the cost of violating the hard margin constraints, i.e., the cost of having some $\xi_i > 0$ is small and therefore the constraint on w dominates. On the contrary, when C is large, classification errors dominate and (P_C) gets closer to (P_0).

4.1.3. Non linear SVM

As noted in the previous section, some classification problems don't have a satisfactory linear solution but have a non linear one. Non linear SVMs are obtained by transforming the original data. Assume given an Hilbert space $\mathcal{H}$ (and denote $\langle .,. \rangle_{\mathcal{H}}$ the corresponding inner product) and a function ϕ from $\mathcal{X}$ to $\mathcal{H}$ (this function is called a *feature map*). A linear SVM in $\mathcal{H}$ can be constructed on the data set $(\phi(x_1), y_1), \ldots, (\phi(x_N), y_N)$. If ϕ is a non linear mapping, the classification rule $(x) = \text{sign}(\langle w, \phi(x) \rangle_{\mathcal{H}} + b)$ is also non linear.

In order to obtain the linear SVM in $\mathcal{H}$ one has to solve the following optimization problem:

$$\begin{aligned} (P_{C,\mathcal{H}})\ &\min_{w,b,\xi} \langle w, w \rangle_{\mathcal{H}} + C \textstyle\sum_{i=1}^{N} \xi_i, \\ &\text{subject to } y_i(\langle w, \phi(x_i) \rangle_{\mathcal{H}} + b) \geq 1 - \xi_i,\ 1 \leq i \leq N, \\ &\xi_i \geq 0,\ 1 \leq i \leq N. \end{aligned}$$

It should be noted that this feature mapping allows to define SVM on almost arbitrary input spaces.

4.1.4. Dual formulation and Kernels

Solving problems (P_C) or $(P_{C,\mathcal{H}})$ might seem very difficult at first, because $\mathcal{X}$ and $\mathcal{H}$ are arbitrary Hilbert spaces and can therefore have very high or even infinite dimension (when $\mathcal{X}$ is a functional space for instance). However, each problem has a dual formulation. More precisely, (P_C) is equivalent to the following optimization problem (see [6]):

$$\begin{aligned} (D_C)\ &\max_{\alpha} \textstyle\sum_{i=1}^{N} \alpha_i - \sum_{i=1}^{N} \sum_{j=1}^{N} \alpha_i \alpha_j y_i y_j \langle x_i, x_j \rangle, \\ &\text{subject to } \textstyle\sum_{i=1}^{N} \alpha_i y_i = 0, \\ &0 \leq \alpha_i \leq C,\ 1 \leq i \leq N. \end{aligned}$$

This result applies to the original problem in which data are not mapped into $\mathcal{H}$, but also to the mapped data, i.e., $(P_{C,\mathcal{H}})$ is equivalent to a problem $(D_{C,\mathcal{H}})$ in which the x_i are replaced by $\phi(x_i)$ and in which the inner product of $\mathcal{H}$ is used. This leads to:

$$\begin{aligned} (D_{C,\mathcal{H}})\ &\max_{\alpha} \textstyle\sum_{i=1}^{N} \alpha_i - \sum_{i=1}^{N} \sum_{j=1}^{N} \alpha_i \alpha_j y_i y_j \langle \phi(x_i), \phi(x_j) \rangle_{\mathcal{H}}, \\ &\text{subject to } \textstyle\sum_{i=1}^{N} \alpha_i y_i = 0, \\ &0 \leq \alpha_i \leq C,\ 1 \leq i \leq N. \end{aligned}$$

Solving $(D_{C,\mathcal{H}})$ rather than $(P_{C,\mathcal{H}})$ has two advantages. The first positive aspect is that $(D_{C,\mathcal{H}})$ is an optimization problem in N rather than in $\mathcal{H}$ which can have infinite dimension (the same is true for $\mathcal{X}$).

The second important point is linked to the fact that the optimal classification rule can be written $(x) = \text{sign}(\sum_{i=1}^{N} \alpha_i y_i \langle \phi(x_i), \phi(x) \rangle_{\mathcal{H}} + b)$. This means that both the optimization problem and the classification rule do not make direct use of the transformed data, i.e. of the $\phi(x_i)$. All the calculations are done through the inner product in $\mathcal{H}$, more precisely through the values $\langle \phi(x_i), \phi(x_j) \rangle_{\mathcal{H}}$. Therefore, rather than choosing directly $\mathcal{H}$ and ϕ, one can provide a so called *Kernel function* K such that $K(x_i, x_j) = \langle \phi(x_i), \phi(x_j) \rangle_{\mathcal{H}}$ for a given pair $(\mathcal{H}, \phi)$.

In order that K corresponds to an actual inner product in a Hilbert space, it has to fulfill some conditions. K has to be symmetric and positive definite, that is, for every N, $x_1, \ldots, x_N$ in $\mathcal{X}$ and $\alpha_1, \ldots, \alpha_N$ in , $\sum_{i=1}^{N} \sum_{j=1}^{N} \alpha_i \alpha_j K(x_i, x_j) \geq 0$. If K satisfies those conditions, according to Moore-Aronszajn theorem [?], there exists a Hilbert space $\mathcal{H}$ and feature map ϕ such that $K(x_i, x_j) = \langle \phi(x_i), \phi(x_j) \rangle_{\mathcal{H}}$.

4.1.5. The case of functional data

The short introduction to SVM proposed in the previous section has clearly shown that defining linear SVM for data in a functional space is as easy as for data in d, because we only assumed that the input space was a Hilbert space. By the dual formulation of the optimization problem (P_C), a software implementation of linear SVM on functional data is even possible, by relying on numerical quadrature methods to calculate the requested integrals (inner product in $L^2(\mu)$, cf section **??**).

However, the functional nature of the data has some effects. It should be first noted that in infinite dimensional Hilbert spaces, the hard margin problem (P_0) has always a solution when the input data are in general positions, i.e., when N observations span a N dimensional subspace of $\mathcal{X}$. A very naive solution would therefore consists in avoiding soft margins and non linear kernels. This would not give very interesting results in practice because of the lack of regularization (see [5] for some examples in very high dimension spaces, as well as section **??**).

Moreover, the linear SVM with soft margin can also lead to bad performances. It is indeed well known (see e.g. [7]) that problem (P_C) is equivalent to the following unconstrained optimization problem:

$$(R_\lambda) \min_{w,b} \frac{1}{N} \sum_{i=1}^{N} \max\left(0, 1 - y_i(\langle w, x_i \rangle + b)\right) + \lambda \langle w, w \rangle,$$

with $\lambda = \frac{1}{CN}$. This way of viewing (P_C) emphasizes the regularization aspect (see also [8–10]) and links the SVM model to ridge regression [?]. As shown in [11], the penalization used in ridge regression behaves poorly with functional data. Of course, the loss function used by SVM (the *hinge loss*, i.e., $h(u, v) = \max(0, 1 - uv)$) is different from the quadratic loss used in ridge regression and therefore no conclusion can be drawn from experiments reported in [11]. However they show that we might expect bad performances with the linear SVM applied directly to functional data. We will see in sections **??** and **??** that the efficiency of the ridge regularization seems to be linked with the actual dimension of the data: it does not behave very well when the number of discretization points is very big and thus leads to approximate the ridge penalty by a dot product in a very high dimensional space (see also section **??**).

It is therefore interesting to consider non linear SVM for functional data, by introducing adapted kernels. As pointed out in e.g. [10], $(P_{C,\mathcal{H}})$ is equivalent to

$$(R_{\lambda,\mathcal{H}}) \min_{f \in \mathcal{H}} \frac{1}{N} \sum_{i=1}^{N} \max\left(0, 1 - y_i f(x_i)\right) + \lambda \langle f, f \rangle_{\mathcal{H}}.$$

Using a kernel corresponds therefore both to replace a linear classifier by a non linear one, but also to replace the ridge penalization by a penalization induced by the kernel which might be more adapted to the problem (see [9] for links between regularization operators and kernels). The applications presented in **??** illustrate this fact.

5. Proposed approach

5.1. Overview of the proposed fusion schema

In this chapter, we propose a new technique in remote-sensing images classification by fusing heterogeneous representations. The proposed approach involve several steps including preprocessing; features extraction; features fusion; matching and classification stages. The block diagram of the proposed technique is shown in Fig. 1. In our previous work [12], we proposed a novel 3D model which design the spectral signature as a three dimensional function which are the time, reflectance, and wavelength band (equation 1). For each pixel, we generated a surface (3D Mesh) which generalizes the usual signature by adding a time dimension. We call this new representation the *multi-temporal spectral signature*. Interested readers can refer to [12].

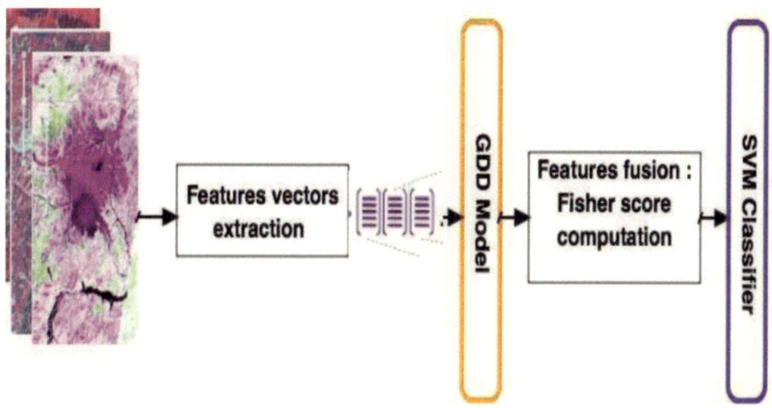

Figure 1. General workflow of the proposed approach

5.2. Images pre-processing and features extraction

In this study multi-temporal hyperspectral images constitutes the source data. Spectral and textural features are the foundational data for this kind of images. The 3D spectral features are extracted from the relative mesh of a given pixel (multi-temporal spectral signature) while the textural ones are derived directly from images. Mainly, two features vectors are generated for each pixel as follows:

Heat kernel signature (HKS) : The HKS is a signature computed only from the intrinsic geometry of an object. Suppose (m, g) is a compelte Riemannian manifold, g is the Riemannian metric. δ is the Laplace-Beltrami operator. The eigenvalues $\{\lambda_n\}$ and eigenfunctions $\{\phi_n\}$ of δ are $\delta\phi_n = \lambda_n\phi_n$, where ϕ_n is normalized to be orthonormal in $L^2(M)$. The Laplace spectrum is given by $0 = \lambda_0 < \lambda_1 \leq \lambda_2 \leq \ldots, \lambda_n \to \infty$. $\triangle$ is the

Laplace-Beltrami operator. As a local shape descriptor, Sun et al. [?] defined the heat kernel signature (HKS) by :

$$h(x,t) = K_{x,t}(x,x) = \sum_{i=0}^{\infty} e^{-\lambda_t} \phi_i^2(x) \tag{25}$$

where $\lambda_0, \lambda_1, \cdots \geq O$ are eigenvalues and $_0, \phi_1, \ldots$ are the corresponding eigenfuctions on the Laplace-Beltrami operator, satisfying $\delta_X \phi_i = \lambda_i \phi_i$. Let's denote this vector by Y.

Spatio-temporal Gabor filters: Texture is one of the important characteristics used in identifying objects or regions of interest. It contains important information about the structural arrangement of surfaces. Fusing texture with 3D spectral information is conducive to the interpretation of remote seeing image [13]. We use a method for dynamic texture modeling based on spatio-temporal Gabor filters. Briefly, the sequence of images is convolved with a bank of spatiotemporal Gabor filters and a feature vector is constructed with the energy of the responses as components. Let's denote this vector by Y'.

5.3. Multi-Features fusion based on a cooperative GDD/SVM classifier

In this section, we present an approach that combines an SVM classifier [1] with a generatively trained GDD model and profits, accordingly, from the advantages of both techniques. The key idea here is to concatenate the extracted features into one vector and to project it in a new space. First, a straightforward feature combination approach is used to concatenate feature vectors (Y and Y') to a single feature vector $X = (X_{i1}, \ldots, X_{idim})$. The *dim* size may differ from one pixel to another making the fusion and classification a challenging tasks. To overcome this limit, we use the Generalized Dirichelet Distribution (GDD) model [14] to map each feature vector into its Fisher score. Therefore, the Fisher kernel function from the GDD is used to replace the Gaussian kernel in the classical SVM.

Let $(X_1, \ldots, X_N)$ denote a collection of N multi-temporal hyperspectral pixels. Each data X_i is assumed to have *dim* size, $X = (X_{i1}, \ldots, X_{idim})$. Each data X_i is assumed to be drawn from the following finite mixture model :

$$p(X_i/\theta) = \sum_{j=1}^{M} p(X_i/j, \theta_j) P(j) \tag{26}$$

where M is the number of components, the $P(j)$, $(0 < P(j) < 1$ and $\sum_{j=1}^{dim} P(j) = 1)$ are the mixing proportions and $p(X/j, \theta_j)$ is the Probability Density Function PDF. θ is the set of parameters to be estimated : $\theta = (\alpha_1, \ldots, \alpha_M, P(1), \ldots, P(M))$.

If the random vector $X = (X_{i1}, \ldots, X_{idim})$ follows a Dirichelet distribution, the joint density function is given by :

$$X = (X_{i1}, \ldots, X_{idim}) = \frac{\tau(|\alpha|)}{\prod_{i=1}^{dim+1} \tau(\alpha_i)} \prod_{i=1}^{dim+1} X_i^{\alpha_i - 1} \tag{27}$$

Since that each feature vector X may has an arbitrary dimension, the proposed method defines the fusion as a projection from one feature vector space (spectral bands) to another with a fixed dimentionnality. Accordingly, the feature-level fusion is done by projecting the vector X combining into one vector in the Fisher space. Thus, the generative model will have its impact on the final classification result through the projection of the extracted features in this new space.

SVM classifier is used to classify the fused features and the multi-temporal dataset of images. Given the generative model obtained by GDD with parameters θ, we compute for each sample X the Fisher score $U_d = \nabla_\theta log P(x|\theta)$ (the gradient of the log likehood of x for model θ). The Fisher kernel operates in the gradient space of the generative mode and provides a natural similarity measure between data samples. For each sample, this score is a vector of fixed dimentionality. Using this score, the Fisher Information matrix is defined as $\mathbb{I} = E_{X_i}\left\{U_{X_i}{}^T U_{X_i}\right\}$. After Fisher score normalization, we compute the Fisher kernel function on the basis of the Euclidean distance between the scores of the new sample and the training samples :

$$K(X, X') = U_{X_i} \mathbb{I}^{-1} U_{X_i'^T} \tag{28}$$

In the second stage, suppose our training set S consists of labels input vectors $(X_i, z_j), i = 1, \ldots, m$ where $X_i \in \mathbb{R}^n$ and $z_i \in \{\pm 1\}$. Given a kernel matrix and a set of labels z_i for each sample, the SVM proceeds to learn a classifier of the form,

$$z(x) = sign(\sum_i \alpha_i z_i) K(X_i, X)) \tag{29}$$

where the coefficients α_i are determined by solving a constrained quadratic program which aims to maximize the margin between the classes. In our experiments we used the LIBSVM package. Our research deals with multi-class problem. The One-Vs-One approach is adopted to extend the proposed approach to multi-temporal hyperspectral classification.

6. Results and discussion

The proposed approach was tested on two different data sets. The datasets involve several types of information with dimensions ranging from 176 to 183 bands. The first dataset, *Hyperion*, contains vegetation type data, is divided into five classes, has 183 spectral bands and has a pixel size of $30m$. The second set is from an airborne sensor (*AVIRIS*), divided into 7 classes, has 176 spectral bands and a pixel size of $18m$. First, we present experiments that assess the classification accuracy of the proposed approach (PA). We also included the direct SVM fusion and a probabilistic fusion approach in our comparison as a baseline. Figure (2) summarizes the results obtained. At each level of label noise we carry out four experiments, and the figures show the mean performance. The strength of this approach is that it combines the rich modeling power of GDD with the discriminative power of the SVM algorithm.

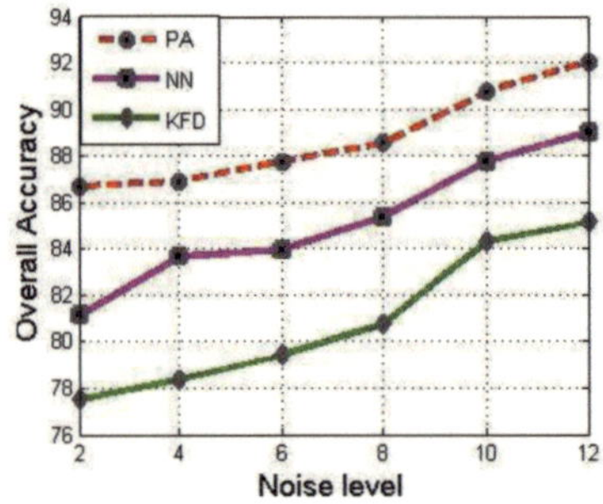

(a) Overall accuracy of the EKFD [Both two sets]

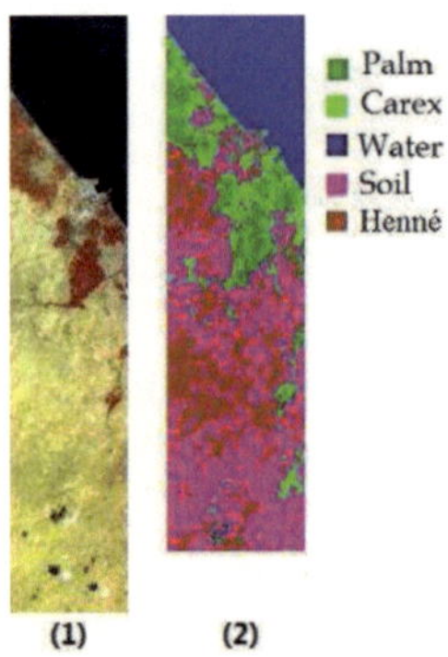

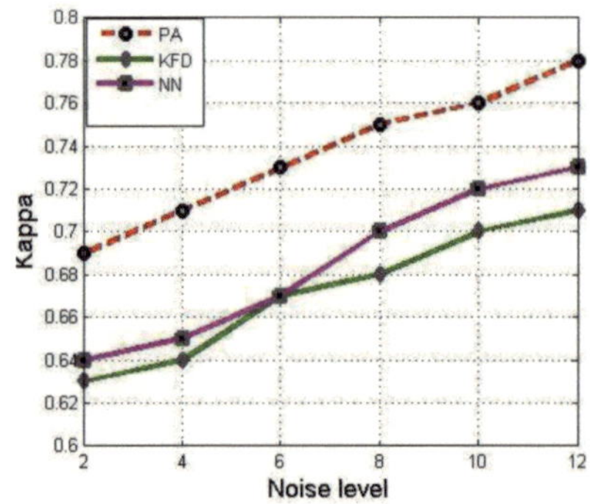

(c) Overall accuracy of the EKFD [Two sets]

(b-1) Map of ground truth
(b-2) Result of classificationwith EKFD [First set]

Figure 2. Experimental results.

Author details

Selim Hemissi and Imed Riadh Farah

RIADII-SIIVT, Tunisia

References

[1] Christopher J. C. Burges. A tutorial on support vector machines for pattern recognition. *Data Min. Knowl. Discov.*, 2(2):121–167, June 1998.

[2] Ilkay Ulusoy and Christopher M Bishop. Comparison of generative and discriminative techniques for object detection and classification. *Toward CategoryLevel Object Recognition*, pages 173–195, 2006.

[3] John Paisley and Lawrence Carin. Dirichlet process mixture models with multiple modalities. In *Acoustics, Speech and Signal Processing, 2009. ICASSP 2009. IEEE International Conference on*, pages 1613–1616, 2009.

http://dx.doi.org/10.5772/56949

[4] Nello Cristianini and John Shawe-Taylor. *An Introduction to Support Vector Machines*. Cambridge University Press, Cambridge, UK, 2000.

[5] Trevor Hastie, Saharon Rosset, Robert Tibshirani, and Ji Zhu. The entire regularization path for the support vector machine. *Journal of Machine Learning Research*, 5:1391–1415, October 2004.

[6] Chih-Jen Lin. Formulations of support vector machines: a note from an optimization point of view. *Neural Computation*, 2(13):307–317, 2001.

[7] Trevor Hastie, Robert Tibshirani, and Jerome Friedman. *The Elements of Statistical Learning: Data Mining, Inference, and Prediction*. Springer-Verlag, 2001.

[8] Alexander Smola and Bernhard SchÅąlkopf. On a kernel-based method for pattern recognition, regression, approximation and operator inversion. *Algorithmica*, 22(1064):211–231, 1998.

[9] Alexander Smola, Bernhard SchÅąlkopf, and Klaus-Robert MÅÿller. The connection between regularization operators and support vector kernels. *Neural Networks*, 11:637–649, 1998.

[10] T. Evgeniou, M. Pontil, and T. Poggio. Regularization networks and support vector machines. *Advances in Computational Mathematics*, 13(1):1–50, 2000.

[11] T. Hastie, A. Buja, and R. Tibshirani. Penalized discriminant analysis. *Annals of Statistics*, 23:73–102, 1995.

[12] Imed Riadh Farah, Selim Hemissi, Karim Saheb Ettabaa, and Bassel Souleiman. Multi-temporal Hyperspectral Images Unmixing and Classification Based on 3D Signature Model and Matching. *Piers Online*, 6:480–484, 2010.

[13] Y Wang and C Chua. Face recognition from 2d and 3d images using 3d gabor filters. *Image and Vision Computing*, 23(11):1018–1028, 2005.

[14] Nizar Bouguila and Djemel Ziou. A dirichlet process mixture of generalized dirichlet distributions for proportional data modeling. *IEEE Transactions on Neural Networks*, 21(1):107–122, 2010.

Chapter 3

Multi-Frequency Image Fusion Based on MIMO UWB OFDM Synthetic Aperture Radar

Md Anowar Hossain, Ibrahim Elshafiey and
Majeed A. S. Alkanhal

Additional information is available at the end of the chapter

http://dx.doi.org/10.5772/56943

1. Introduction

The principle idea behind synthetic aperture radar (SAR) stems from the desire for high-resolution images. SAR transmits signal at spaced intervals called pulse repetition interval (PRI). The responses at each PRI are collected and processed to reconstruct a radar image of the terrain [1]. In general, high-resolution SAR images in range domain are generated using ultra-wideband (UWB) waveforms as radar transmitted pulse [2]. UWB pulses (500 MHz bandwidth and above) can enhance the range resolution considerably. UWB technology has dual advantages: good capacity of penetration and high-resolution target detection in range domain for radar applications [3].

Orthogonal frequency division multiplexing (OFDM), a modulation scheme commonly utilized in commercial communications, shows a great potential for use in forming radar waveforms. An OFDM signal is comprised of several orthogonal subcarriers, which are simultaneously emitted over a single transmission path. Each subcarrier occupies a small slice of the entire signal bandwidth [4]. Technology advances helped in increasing the sampling speed capabilities, allowing accurate generation of UWB-OFDM waveforms. This results in a diverse signal that is capable of high-resolution imaging. While OFDM has been elaborately studied and commercialized in the digital communication field, it has not yet been widely studied by the radar scientific community apart from a few efforts [5-7]. The advantages of using OFDM in radar applications include: (a) Transceiver system is based on digital implementation using relatively inexpensive components (b) Ease of narrowband interference mitigation (c) High-resolution in UWB scale and good multi-path potential (d) Same architecture can be used to transmit large amounts of data in real time; and (e) Flexibility in pulse shaping using different subcarrier compositions.

Although SAR is a well-known remote sensing application which obtains high-resolution in range domain by transmitting wide-band waveform and high-resolution in azimuth domain by utilizing the relative motion between the target and the radar platform, current single antenna SAR is not able to provide some remote sensing performances, such as simultaneously high-resolution and wide-swath imaging. Multiple-Input Multiple-Output (MIMO) SAR provides a solution to resolve these problems and provides following advantages compared to traditional SAR: diversity in viewing angles on a particular target to improve identifiability, increased azimuth resolution or decreased pulse repetition frequency (PRF) which results in wider swath. Due to the larger number of degrees-of-freedom of a MIMO system, enhanced resolution can be achieved by coherently processing of multiple waveforms at multiple receivers simultaneously.

Several research works have been reported in recent years to overcome the trade-off between wide-swath and azimuth resolution in conventional SAR system [8]. However, MIMO SAR systems are only investigated by generalizing the theoretical modeling of MIMO communication systems and discussed recently in radar communities [9 and 10]. The configuration of the proposed MIMO-SAR system in this chapter is considered as two co-located transmitters and two receivers along with image fusion technique.

In remote sensing applications, the increasing availability of spaceborne sensor gives a motivation to utilize image fusion algorithms. Several situations in image processing require high spatial and high spectral resolution in a single image. Image fusion is the process of combining relevant information from two or more images into a single image. The resulting image will be more informative than any of the input images [11].

The structure of the chapter is as follows. UWB-OFDM pulse shaping for MIMO SAR is described in section 2, while the comparison of auto-correlation and cross-correlation of different pulses in radar perspective is presented in section 3. Detailed analysis of MIMO wide-swath SAR system and its functionality is discussed in section 4. MIMO wide-swath SAR imaging results based on UWB-OFDM waveforms are presented in section 5. Section 6 presents the optimized SAR image based on image fusion technique. Final conclusions are provided in section 7.

2. MIMO UWB OFDM signal generation

A widely studied approach in MIMO architecture involves the transmission of orthogonal signals from different antennas. This makes it possible to separate the reflected signals from the target arriving at the receiver. In particular, we develop a procedure to design the optimal waveform that ensures orthogonality by imposing the rules shown in Table 1. The key to our approach is to use a model for the received radar signals that explicitly includes the transmitted waveforms. To achieve lower cross-correlation between transmitted pulses with a common bandwidth for the same range resolution, OFDM frequency-domain sample vector for N subcarriers is generated using the sequences shown in Table 1. The sequence in Table 1 generates the orthogonal signals based on the placement of 1's and 0's. We observe that in each column, if we consider a 1, the other elements are 0's and the next column is filled with all 0's to prevent over-sampling. The spectrum of an OFDM signal is shown in Figure 1 where the width of the main-lobe depends on the duration of the pulse. In digital implementation of an OFDM signal, the pulse duration is related to the number of subcarriers. As the number of subcarrier increases, the duration of the pulse increases.

	1	2	3	-	-	-	-	-	-	-	-	-	-	-	-	N
$\Psi_{\omega1}$	1	0	0	0	0	0	0	0	1	0	0	0	0	0	0	0
$\Psi_{\omega2}$	0	0	1	0	0	0	0	0	0	0	1	0	0	0	0	0
$\Psi_{\omega3}$	0	0	0	0	1	0	0	0	0	0	0	0	1	0	0	0
$\Psi_{\omega4}$	0	0	0	0	0	0	1	0	0	0	0	0	0	0	1	0

Table 1. OFDM frequency-domain sample vector generation

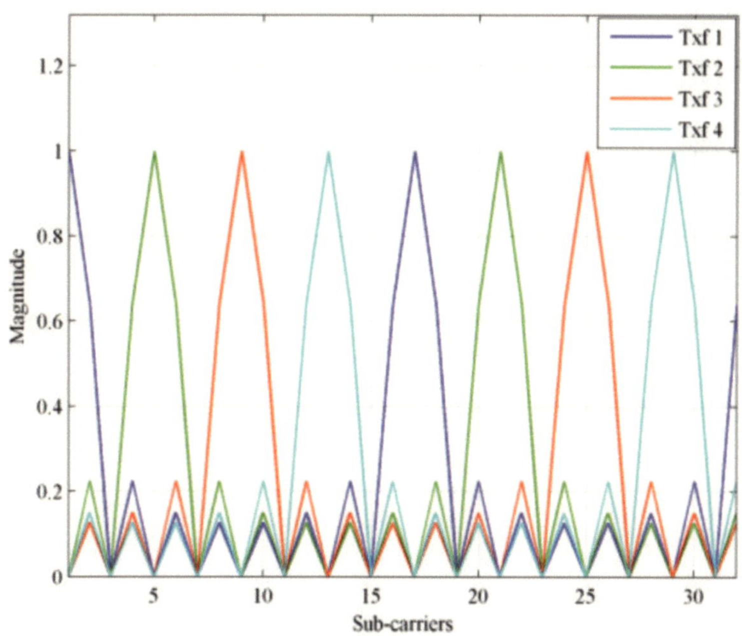

Figure 1. OFDM signal spectrum

As an example, an OFDM signal is generated according to the scheme shown in Figure 2 by spreading the digital frequency domain vector shown in Table 1 and the modulation symbol from random integer generator. The order of modulation (M) is chosen as 4 for QPSK. Inverse Fast Fourier Transform (IFFT) is then applied to obtain the discrete time domain OFDM signal and finally Hanning window is imposed to minimize the side-lobes. The time-domain OFDM signal is given as

$$\Psi_{txi}(t) = F^{-1}[\Psi_{\omega i}]\, w(n) \qquad i = 1, 2, \cdots 4 \tag{1}$$

where, Hanning window $w(n) = 0.5\left\{1 - cos\left(\frac{2\pi n}{N}\right)\right\}$, $0 \le n \le N - 1$ and N is the number of subcarriers. The term $\Psi_{\omega i}$ denotes the spreading sequences for i^{th} sub-pulses. Each antenna transmits two sub-pulses simultaneously.

UWB-OFDM waveforms are generated using the following parameters: number of OFDM subcarriers, $N = 256$, sampling time, $\Delta t_s = 1$ns results in baseband bandwidth, $B_0 = 1/2\Delta t_s = 500$ MHz, dividing by a factor of two to satisfy Nyquist criterion. UWB-OFDM waveform in frequency domain and time domain is shown in Figure 3 and Figure 4 respectively. We can observe that the Hanning window reasonably minimizes side-lobes which in turns improve the auto-correlation function (ACF) and cross-correlation function (CCF) of time-domain OFDM waveforms as shown in Figure 5 and Figure 6, respectively.

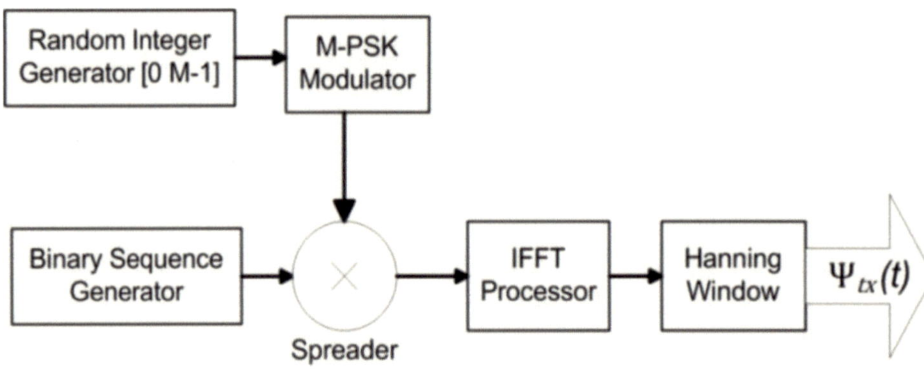

Figure 2. OFDM signal generator

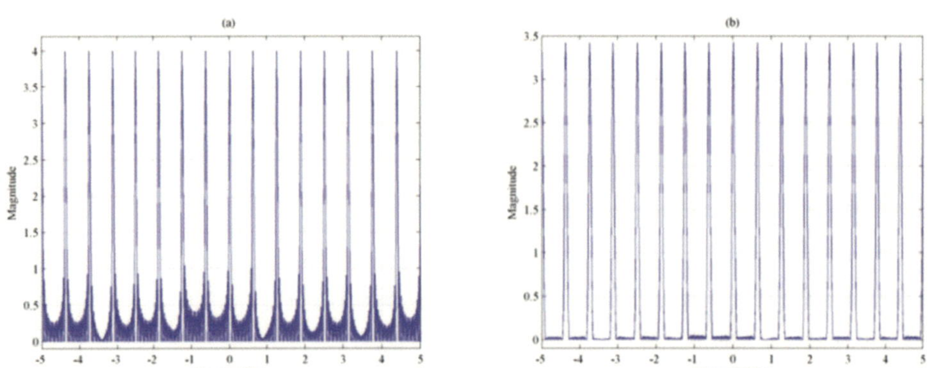

Figure 3. UWB-OFDM waveform in frequency-domain (a) before windowing (b) after windowing

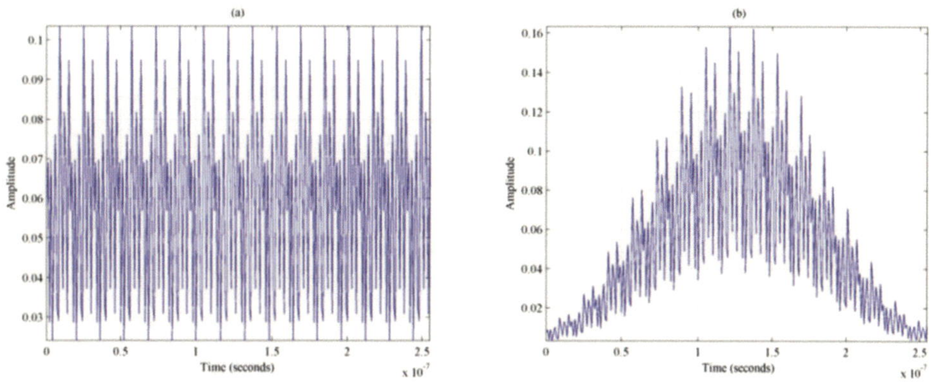

Figure 4. UWB-OFDM waveform in time-domain (a) before windowing (b) after windowing

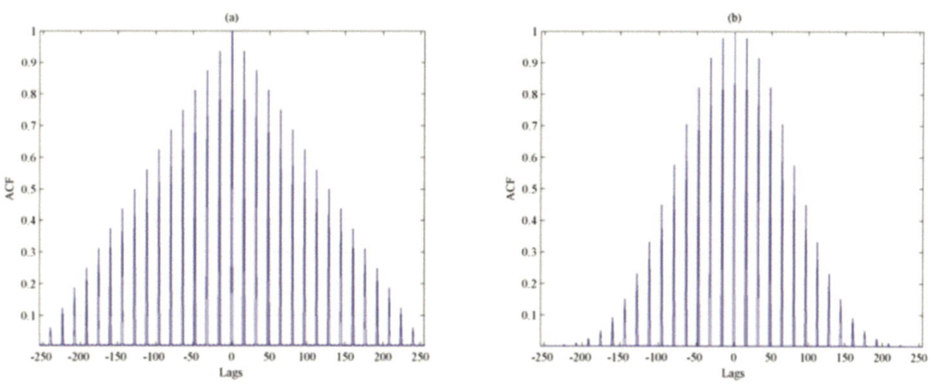

Figure 5. Auto-correlation function (ACF) of OFDM pulses in time domain (a) before windowing (b) after windowing

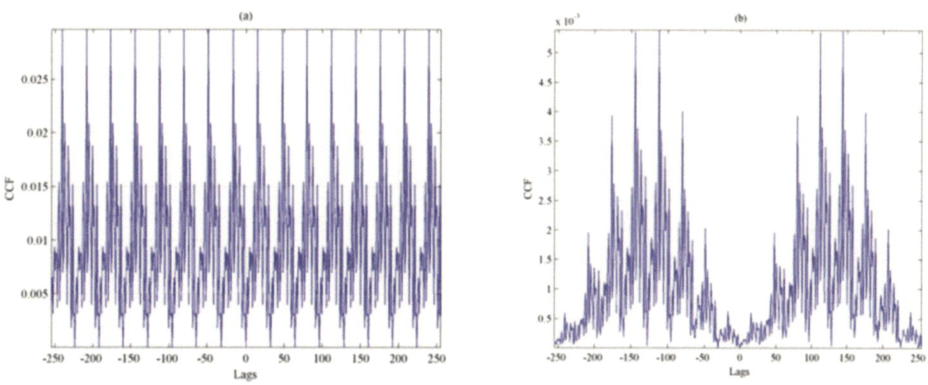

Figure 6. Cross-correlation function (CCF) of OFDM pulses in time domain (a) before windowing (b) after windowing

3. Comparison of auto-correlation and cross-correlation

Cross-correlation is the measure of similarity between two different sequences and can be given as

$$R_{xy}(m) = \begin{cases} \sum_{n=0}^{N-m-1} x_{n+m} y_n^* & m \ge 0 \\ R_{yx}^*(-m) & m < 0 \end{cases} \quad (2)$$

where, x_n and y_n are the elements of two different sequences and have period N. Auto-correlation shows the measure of similarity between the sequence and its cyclic shifted copy can be obtained from equation (2) as a special case $(x = y)$ [12].

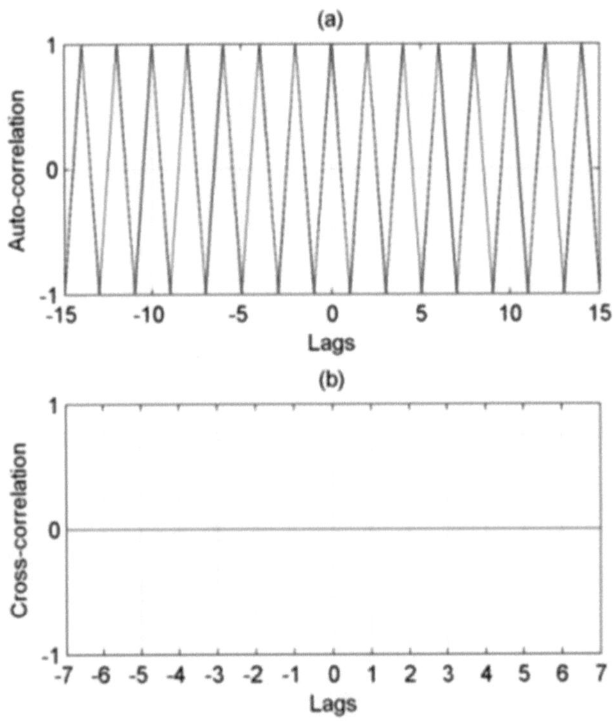

Figure 7. Ideal Walsh-Hadamard sequences (a) ACF (b) CCF

The auto-correlation and cross-correlation properties of the sequences used in generating the transmitted waveform play an important role in high-resolution SAR imaging based on MIMO architecture. Practically, lower cross-correlation between waveforms avoids interference which results in independent information gains from target signature at various angles. Similarly, low auto-correlation peak side-lobe ratio ensures high-resolution in range domain.

http://dx.doi.org/10.5772/56943

Thus, the waveforms with lower cross-correlation and auto-correlation peak side-lobe are desired for MIMO SAR systems. The sequences with good auto-correlation property provide high-resolution target detection and lower cross-correlation mitigates the interference from nearby sensors.

Orthogonality is the most important properties of Walsh-Hadamard sequences [12]. Because of this property, the cross-correlation between any two codes of the same set is zero as shown in Figure 7. Unfortunately, Walsh sequences are orthogonal only in the case of perfect synchronization, and have non-zero off-peak auto-correlations and cross–correlation in asynchronous case. To compare the performance of OFDM signal using Walsh-Hadamard sequences and proposed orthogonal sequences for radar application, we can analyze ACF and CCF by assuming a point target at the center of the target area.

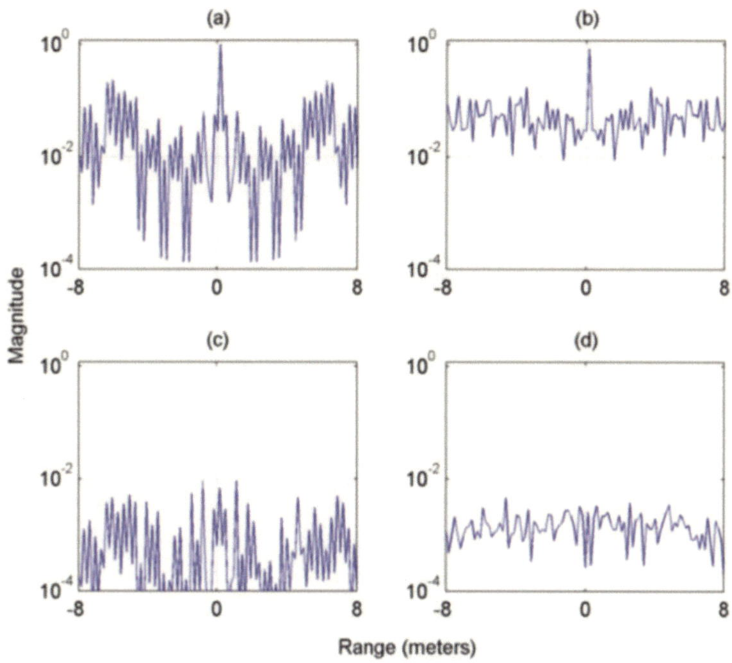

Figure 8. Point target profile using Walsh-Hadamard sequences and proposed orthogonal sequences (a) ACF of Walsh-Hadamard (b) ACF of proposed orthogonal sequences (c) CCF of Walsh-Hadamard (d) CCF of proposed orthogonal sequences

Figure 8(a) and Figure 8(b) show the auto-correlation, while Figure 8(c) and Figure 8(d) show the cross-correlation in terms of a point target using Walsh-Hadamard sequences and proposed orthogonal sequences respectively. The auto-correlation is measured as the correlation between the received signal and the transmitted signal at same antenna, while cross-correlation is measured as the correlation between transmitted signal in one antenna and the received signal in another antenna. We can observe that the significant improvement in ACF and CCF for a point target profile using proposed orthogonal pulses in comparison with Walsh-

Hadamard sequences. In MIMO SAR, ACF between transmitted and received signal of the same antenna should provide narrow main-lobe width for high-resolution. Lower CCF properties between transmitted signal of one antenna and received signal of another antenna are needed to avoid interference from nearby sensor. The main-lobe width of the proposed sequence shown in Figure 8(b) is reasonably narrow in comparison with Figure 8(a) which in turns improves the range resolution. In case of CCF, since all cross-correlation values, not just peak values, affect the system performance, we should consider the measure as mean cross-correlation value. The mean CCF of the proposed sequence shown in Figure 8 (d) is much lower than the Walsh-Hadamard sequence shown in Figure 8(c).

4. MIMO wide-swath SAR imaging system

In MIMO SAR, independent signals are transmitted through different antennas, and these signals are received by multiple antennas after propagating through the environment. Each antenna transmits a unique waveform orthogonal to the waveforms transmitted by other antennas; the returns of each orthogonal signal will carry independent information about the targets. In the receiver, a matched filter-bank is used to extract the orthogonal waveform components. Consider the MIMO SAR system with a transmit array equipped with 2 co-located antennas and a receive array (possibly the same array) equipped with 2 co-located antennas. Suppose both transmit and receive arrays are close to each other in space but they see different target area at different directions. Figure 9 shows the MIMO wide-swath stripmap SAR imaging topology and Figure 10 shows the block diagram of the MIMO OFDM SAR imaging system.

The antenna beam A and B are illuminating the swath *A* and *B* respectively. At an specific PRI, *TxA* transmits pulse $\Psi_{txA}(t)$ via the antenna beam *A*, while *TxB* transmits the pulse $\Psi_{txB}(t)$ via the antenna beam B at the same time. Echoes from swath *A* and *B* will exist at the both receivers. To separate echoes from swath *A* and *B*, a careful design of transmit antenna pattern as well as transmitted pulse is required. It can further reduce the disturbance echoes from the temporal undesired swath.

The OFDM signal generator generates signal according to the scheme shown in Figure 2. The detailed of the block diagram components such as D/A converter, mixer and power amplifier shown in Figure 10 can be found in [5]. We consider four typical orthogonal sub-pulses based on the sample vectors shown in Table 1. Two different signals $\Psi_{txA}(t)$ and $\Psi_{txB}(t)$ are transmitted simultaneously from antenna *A* and *B* respectively at each PRI where each signal is the combination of two sub-pulses and are given as

$$\Psi_{txA}(t) = \Psi_{tx1}(t) + \Psi_{tx2}(t) \tag{3}$$

$$\Psi_{txB}(t) = \Psi_{tx3}(t) + \Psi_{tx4}(t) \tag{4}$$

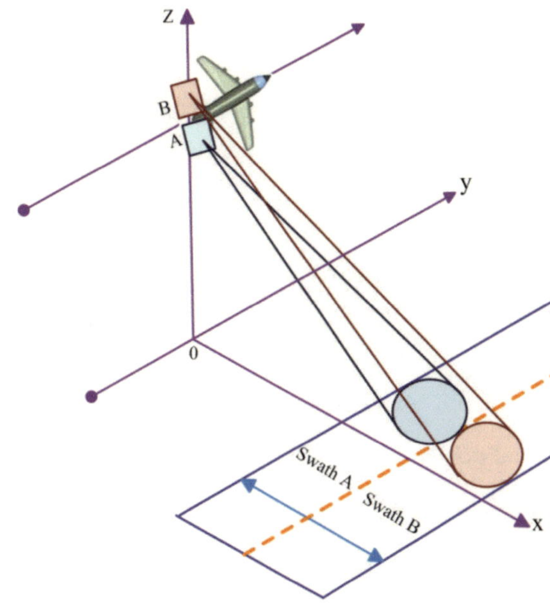

Figure 9. MIMO stripmap wide-swath SAR imaging topology

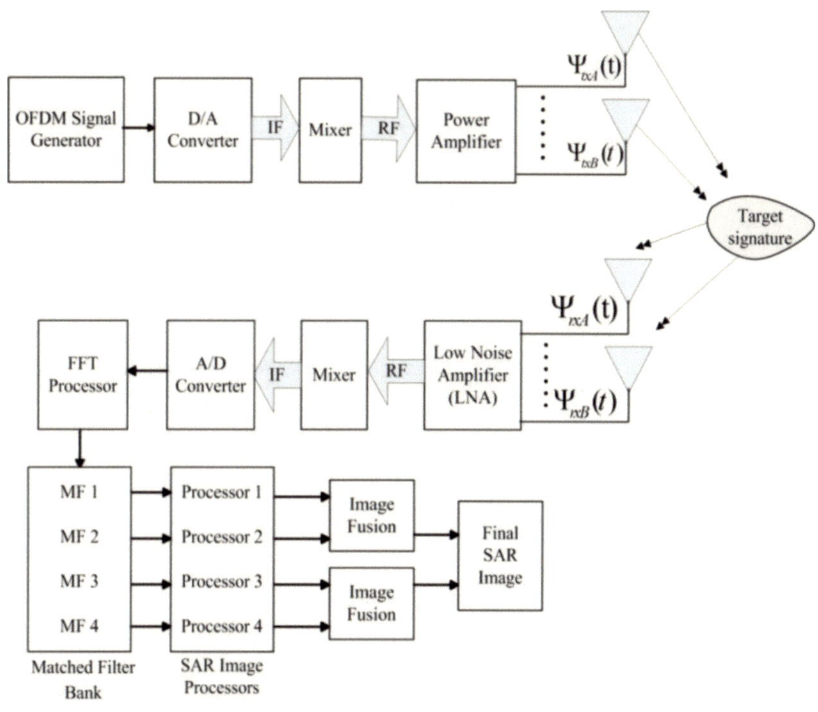

Figure 10. MIMO OFDM SAR imaging system

The received signal for radar at antenna A is given by

$$\Psi_{rxA}(t,u)=\alpha\left[\sum_{n=1}^{N}\sigma_n\Psi_{txA}(t-t_{dnA})\right]+\beta\left[\sum_{n=1}^{N}\sigma_n\Psi_{txB}(t-t_{dnB})\right]+\eta_A(t) \tag{5}$$

Similarly, the received signal at antenna B is given as

$$\Psi_{rxB}(t,u)=\alpha\left[\sum_{n=1}^{N}\sigma_n\Psi_{txB}(t-t_{dnB})\right]+\beta\left[\sum_{n=1}^{N}\sigma_n\Psi_{txA}(t-t_{dnA})\right]+\eta_B(t) \tag{6}$$

where, α and β are the scale factor and is chosen as $\frac{1}{\sqrt{2}}$ and $\frac{1}{\sqrt{10}}$ respectively. The scale factor α is chosen to distribute the total power to two sub-pulses and β is chosen to model the out-of-beam signal. The term $t_{dnA}=\frac{2}{c}\sqrt{(X_{cA}+x_n)^2+(y_n-u)^2}$ is the time-delay associated with the target position (x_n, y_n) in swath A and $t_{dnB}=\frac{2}{c}\sqrt{(X_{cB}+x_n)^2+(y_n-u)^2}$ is the time-delay associated with swath B. X_{cA} and X_{cB} denote the range distance to the center of the swath A and B respectively, where, $n = 1, 2, 3\ldots N$ are the number of targets within the antenna beam at any given synthetic aperture position (u) in azimuth direction while σ_n denotes the reflectivity of the nth target. The terms $\eta_A(t)$ and $\eta_B(t)$ denote the additive white Gaussian noise.

Next, the received radar echoes should be separated apart by matched filtering. As the transmitted signal matrix is known to both transmitter and receiver and the transmitted waveforms are designed to be orthogonal, they should satisfy the conditions

$$\int_0^{T_p}\Psi_{rxm}(t)\Psi^*_{txn}(t)=\begin{cases}\delta(t), & m=n\\ 0, & m\neq n\end{cases} \tag{7}$$

where, T_p is the sub-pulse duration and $(.)^*$ denotes a conjugate operator. At receiving antenna A, two received orthogonal sub-pulses can be extracted by two matched filters and is given by

$$\Psi_{MFn}(t)=F^{-1}\left[F\{\Psi_{rxA}(t)\}.F\{\Psi^*_{txn}(t)\}\right] \tag{8}$$

Similarly, at receiving antenna B, two sub-pulses can be separated as

$$\Psi_{MFn}(t)=F^{-1}\left[F\{\Psi_{rxB}(t)\}.F\{\Psi^*_{txn}(t)\}\right] \tag{9}$$

where, $n = 1, 2$ for equation (8) and $n = 3, 4$ for equation (9) while F^{-1} and F denote the inverse Fourier transform and Fourier transform operations respectively. Therefore, echoes from different swaths could be considered as well separated after the matched filtering.

Finally, we will have a total of four extracted signals from two receiving antennas. Compared to the traditional phased array SAR where the same waveform is used at all the transmitting antennas and a total of 2 coefficients are obtained from the matched filtering, the MIMO OFDM SAR gives more coefficients and therefore provides more degrees of freedom [8]. Each matched filter output is then processed separately using SAR imaging algorithms such as Range-Doppler algorithm and image fusion technique is then applied to achieve final SAR reconstructed image as described in the following sections.

5. MIMO Wide-swath SAR Imaging

The scenario involves the wide-swath SAR imaging by considering four distinct orthogonal UWB-OFDM sub-pulses as SAR transmitted signals using two antennas. The objective is to investigate the performance of the proposed orthogonal waveforms in MIMO architecture. Let us consider 2 point targets reside in swath A at the positions $[(x_1, y_1), (x_2, y_2)] = [(300, 100), (900, -50)]$ while 2 point targets reside at the positions $[(x_3, y_3), (x_4, y_4)] = [(300, -50), (900, 100)]$ in swath B. Stripmap SAR imaging topology is considered for raw data generation based on the proposed UWB-OFDM waveforms [5] while Range-Doppler algorithm is used for SAR image reconstruction [13 and 14]. Processing of SAR raw data from multiple antennas can be done in parallel. Field Programmable Gate Array (FPGA) is a powerful tool for real-time implementation of SAR image reconstruction from raw data [15 and 16]. Figure 11 and Figure 12 show the resolved images of swath A based on the output of matched filter 1 and 2 respectively while Figure 13 and Figure 14 show the reconstructed images of swath B based on the output of matched filter 3 and 4.

6. Image fusion

Observing a given scene from two SAR antennas with distinct trajectories allows one to determine the position of the scattering points. Unfortunately, SAR interferometry fails when the scenes imaged by the two antennas are not really the same scene, due to a too large distance between the trajectories of the two SAR antennas. In these cases, the two images may not be sufficiently correlated. SAR image fusion is presented here exploiting the data recorded by same antennas about the same scene using two sub-pulses simultaneously. The usefulness of the fusion technique is evaluated by estimating the noise level for the non-fused and the fused images in terms of entropy. In addition, the behavior of the back-scatterer, as a function of frequency, changes on the basis of the surface types. Therefore, if the images acquired in many regions of the spectrum are fused, the output image will carry useful information about specific back-scatterers. Furthermore, the fusion of multi-frequency images can allow us to fuse the information acquired about the object observed in many spectral bands, in the same spatial context. Complementary information about the same observed scene can be available in the following cases:– data recorded by the same sensor scanning the same scene at different dates (multi-temporal image fusion); – data recorded by the same sensor operating in different spectral bands (multi-frequency image fusion); – data recorded by the same sensor at different polarizations (multi-polarization image fusion); – data recorded by the same sensor located on platforms flying at different heights (multi-resolution image fusion).

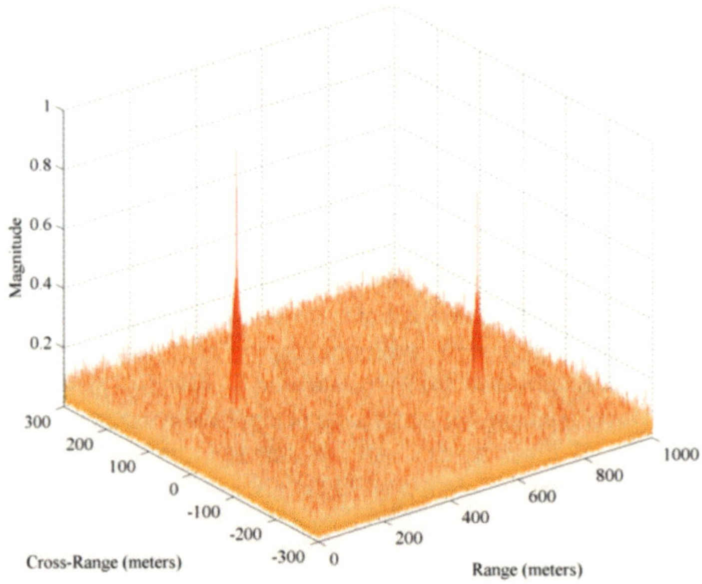

Figure 11. Reconstructed image from matched filter 1 (swath A)

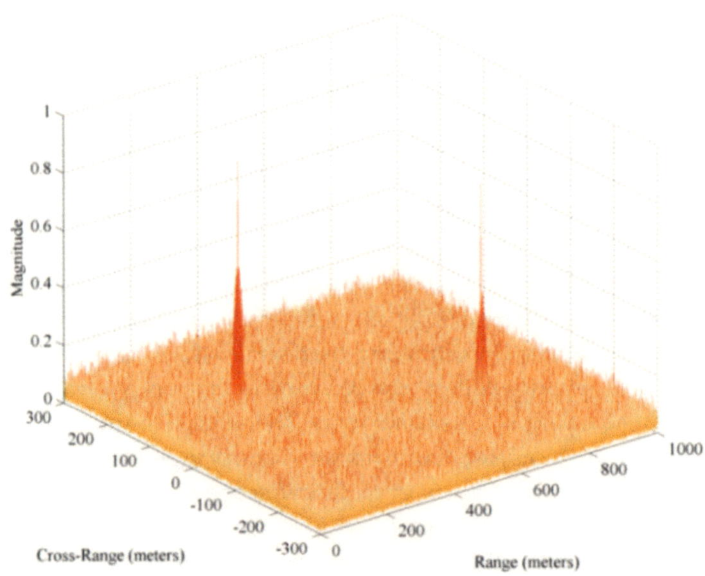

Figure 12. Reconstructed image from matched filter 2 (swath A)

Many methods exist to perform image fusion. The very basic one is based on discrete wavelet transform (DWT) has become a very useful tool for fusion. DWT is a wavelet transform for which the wavelets are discretely sampled. As with other wavelet transforms, a key advantage it has over Fourier transforms is temporal resolution: it captures both frequency and location information (location in time). Figure 15 shows the block diagram of wavelet transform based image fusion technique. The principle of image fusion using wavelets is to merge the wavelet decompositions of the two original images using fusion methods applied to approximations coefficients and details coefficients [11]. The DWT is a spatial frequency decomposition that provides a flexible multi-resolution analysis of an image. The inverse discrete wavelet transform (IDWT) is applied to the combined coefficient map to produce the fused image from the two input images.

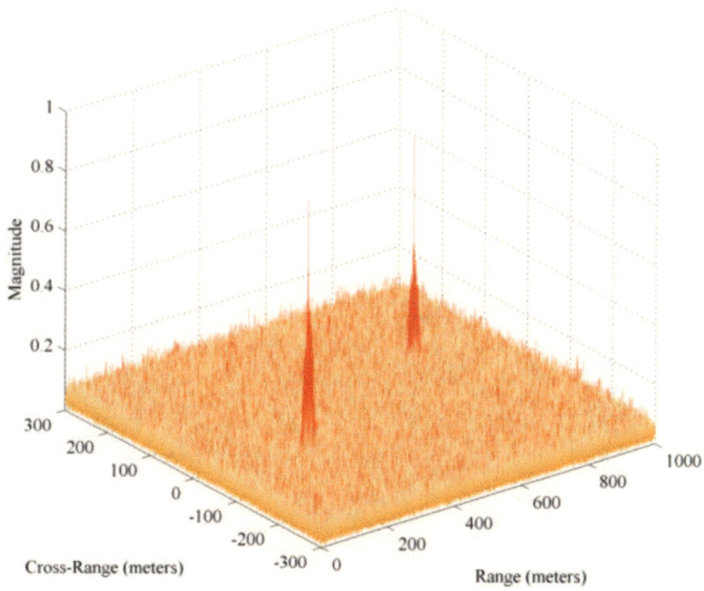

Figure 13. Reconstructed image of matched filter 3 (swath B)

In all wavelet based image fusion schemes the DWT of the two registered input images $I_1(x, y)$ and $I_2(x, y)$ are computed and these transforms are combined using some kind of fusion rule. Then the inverse discrete wavelet transform (IDWT) is computed and the fused image $I(x, y)$ is reconstructed as

$$I(x, y)=W^{-1}[\phi\{W(I_1(x, y)), W(I_2(x, y))\}] \tag{10}$$

where, W and W^{-1} denotes the DWT and IDWT respectively. The term ϕ denotes the rules imposed in fusion such as wavelet function, level, approximation, and detail coefficients. Figure 16 shows the single level decomposition of the image shown in Figure 14 using Haar wavelet function.

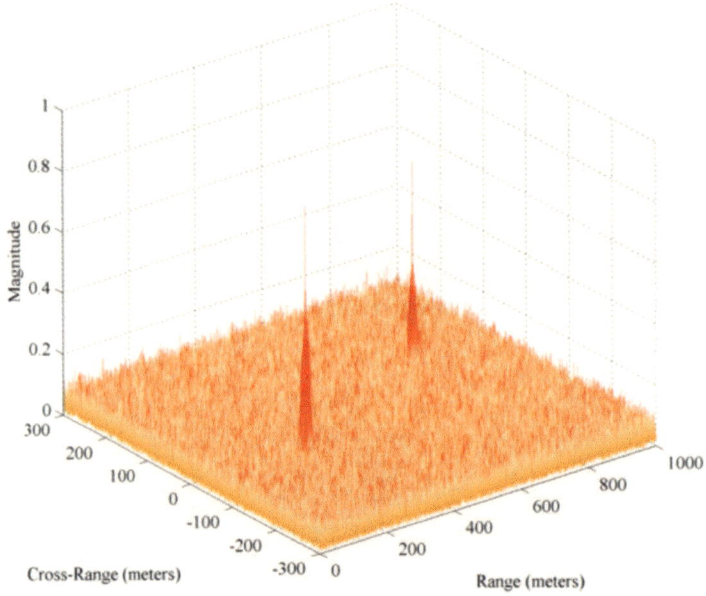

Figure 14. Reconstructed image of matched filter 4 (swath B)

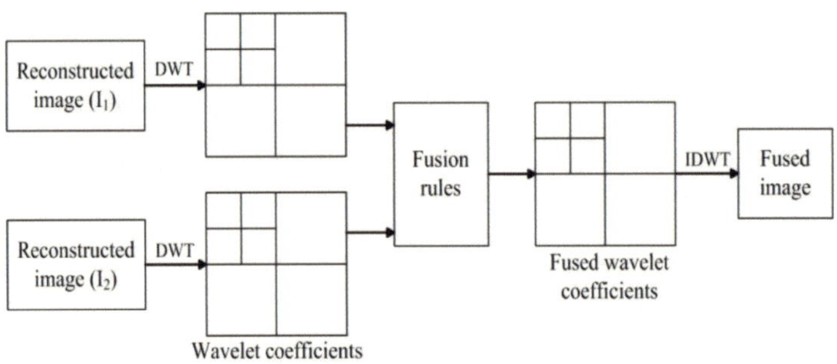

Figure 15. Wavelet transform based image fusion

Figure 17 shows the fused image obtained using the reconstructed images from matched filters 1 and 2 while Figure 18 shows the fused image using the reconstructed images from matched filters 3 and 4. The image fusion output shown in Figure 17 and Figure 18 is achieved by taking the 'maximum' for 'approximations' and the 'minimum' for the 'details' using level 5 based on Haar wavelet. Haar wavelet is chosen because of its simplicity and good reconstruction capability. Since wavelet coefficients with large absolute values contain the information about the salient features of the images such as edges and lines, a good fusion rule is to choose the 'maximum' for 'approximation' values, while 'minimum' is chosen for the 'details' to suppress the noise. Final reconstructed wide-swath SAR image shown in Figure 19 with all resolved point targets of swath A and B is the horizontal concatenation of fused images of Figure 17 and Figure 18.

http://dx.doi.org/10.5772/56943

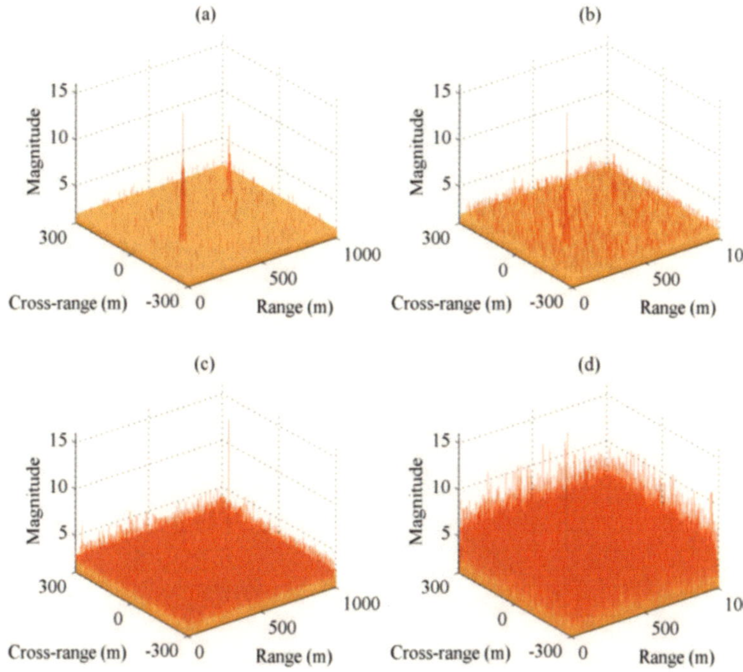

Figure 16. Single level decomposition (a) Approximation (b) Horizontal detail (c) Vertical detail (d) Diagonal detail

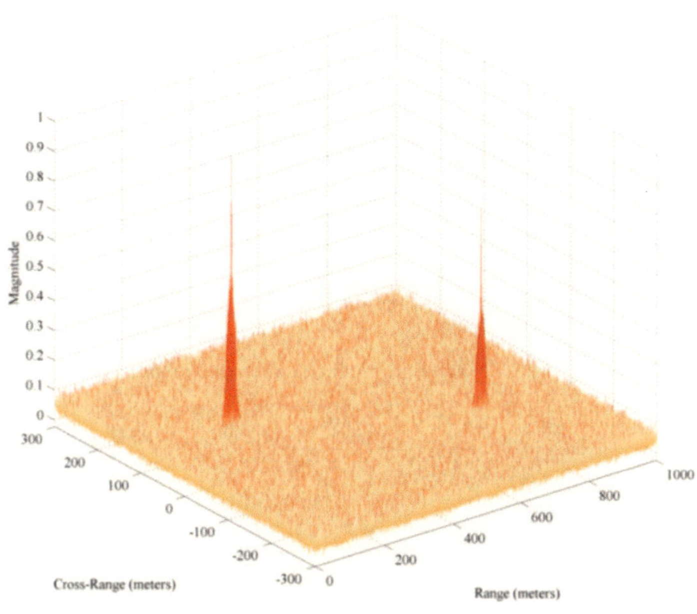

Figure 17. Fused image of swath A

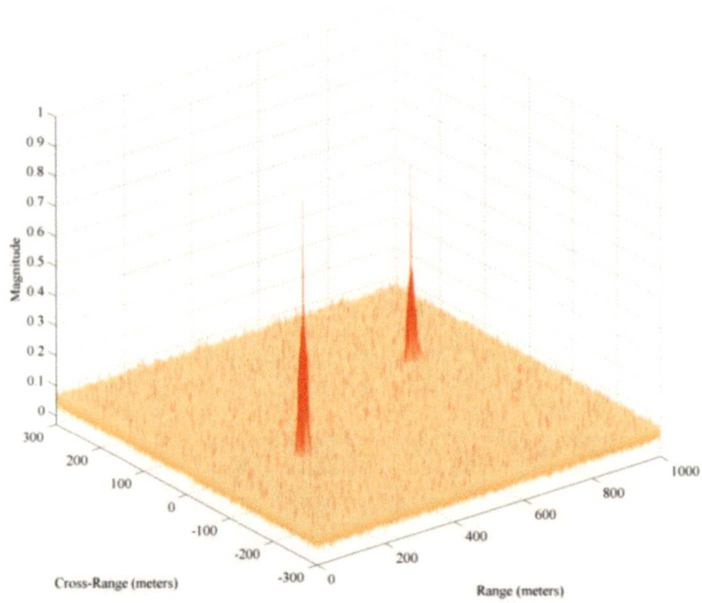

Figure 18. Fused Image of Swath B

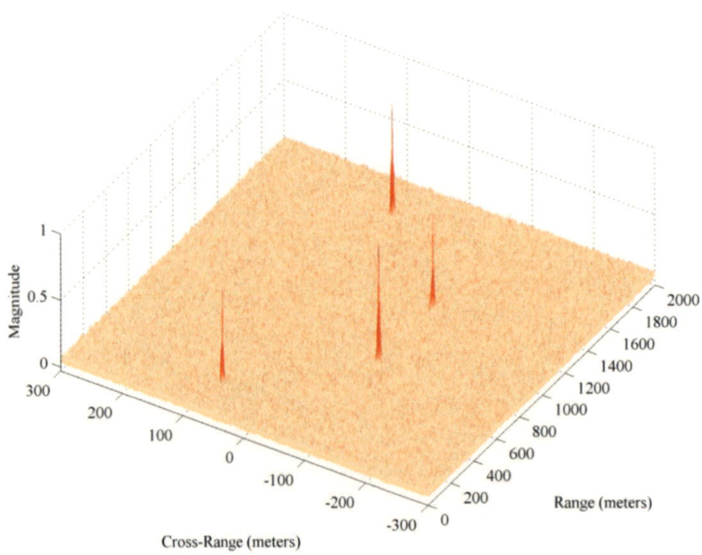

Figure 19. Final SAR image

To assess the reduction in noise level due to image fusion technique, we can analyze both input images and fused image in terms of entropy. Entropy is a good measure for information content (uncertainty) present in the image space. Information content in SAR images after wavelet transform based image fusion is identified with entropy value that serves as a measure of the roughness present in the image space. Entropy is used as a metric of noise level in non-fused and fused images. Table 2 summarizes the entropy of the input images of swath A and B as well as the fused images for different wavelet families. We observe that the Haar wavelet gives the best reduction in noise level.

Wavelet	Parameters	Entropy of image 1	Entropy of image 2	Entropy of fused image (Swath A)	Entropy of fused image (Swath B)
Haar	Level : 5 Approx.: Max Details: Min	(Swath A) 4.6353 (Swath B) 4.5606	(Swath A) 4.6072 (Swath B) 4.5362	3.9572	3.8627
Daubechies1				3.9574	3.8630
Symlets2				3.9594	3.8696
Coiflets2				3.9605	3.8723

Table 2. Entropy of fused SAR images using different wavelet families.

7. Conclusions

An image fusion based MIMO UWB-OFDM SAR system has been presented which is able to provide wide-swath imaging. Pulse shaping is an important component in OFDM applications. As orthogonal transmission waveforms are required for the proposed MIMO OFDM SAR system, a new approach to generate OFDM waveforms is explored and investigated. It is shown that the proposed MIMO UWB-OFDM SAR indeed provides a potential solution to high-resolution remote sensing as well as wide-swath imaging. The usefulness of the developed approach has been demonstrated by fusing SAR images. Image fusion techniques provide a powerful tool to reduce clutter and certain types of noise such as AWGN, and thus can be used to enhance the quality of SAR images. The performance of the system is estimated by testing the proposed technique on SAR data acquired on multiple sensors. The results are evaluated by estimating the information flow from the input data to the output image, in terms of automatic recognition and detection of features present in the acquired images. Each SAR sensor acquires data about the inspected region using more than one frequency, and a processor that exploits the information carried by multiple frequencies is thus needed. Future work may include investigation of the proposed system by exploiting sensors that scan the from multiple heights using various platforms.

Acknowledgements

This work is funded by the National Plan for Science and Technology, Kingdom of Saudi Arabia, under project number: 08-ELE262-2.

Author details

Md Anowar Hossain*, Ibrahim Elshafiey and Majeed A. S. Alkanhal

*Address all correspondence to: ahossain@ksu.edu.sa

Electrical Engineering Department, King Saud University, Riyadh, Kingdom of Saudi Arabia

References

[1] Soumekh M. Synthetic Aperture Radar Signal Processing with MATLAB Algorithms. New York: Wiley, 1999.

[2] Lim B-G, Woo J-C, Lee H-Y, and Kim Y-S. A Modified Subpulse SAR Processing Procedure Based on the Range-Doppler Algorithm for Synthetic Wideband Waveforms. *Sensors*, 8, pp.8224-8236, 2008.

[3] Aiello R. and Wood S. Essentials of UWB. New York: Cambridge, 2008.

[4] Hanzo L. and Keller T. OFDM and MC-CDMA. West Sussex: Wiley, 2006.

[5] Hossain M. A., Elshafiey I., Alkanhal M., and Mabrouk A. Adaptive UWB-OFDM Synthetic Aperture Radar. *Proc. of Saudi International Electronics, Communications and Photonics Conference (SIECPC)*, Riyadh, Saudi Arabia, pp. 1-6, 2011.

[6] Hossain M. A., Elshafiey I., and Alkanhal M. High-resolution UWB SAR based on OFDM architecture. *Proc. of 3rd Asia-Pacific International Conference on Synthetic Aperture Radar (APSAR)*. Seoul, South Korea, pp.1-4, 2011.

[7] Hossain M. A., Elshafiey I., Alkanhal M., and Mabrouk A. Anti-jamming Capabilities of UWB-OFDM SAR. *Proc. of European Radar Conference (EuRad)*, Manchester, United Kingdom, pp.313-316, 2011.

[8] Wang W-Q. Space-Time Coding MIMO-OFDM SAR for High-Resolution Imaging. *IEEE Trans. on Geosciences and Remote Sensing*, 49(8), pp.3094-3104, 2011.

[9] Lim S. H., Hwang C. G., Kim S. Y., and Myung N H. Shifting MIMO SAR System for High-resolution Wide-swath Imaging. *Journal of Electromagnetic Waves and Applications (JEMWA)*, 25, pp.1168-1178, 2011.

[10] Xu W., Huang P. P., and Deng Y. K. MIMO-Tops Mode for High-resolution Ultra-Wide-Swath Full Polarimetric Imaging," *Progress in Electromagnetics Research (PIER)*, 121, pp.19-37, 2011.

[11] Zeeuw P. M. Wavelet and Image Fusion. Amsterdam: CWI, 1998.

http://dx.doi.org/10.5772/56943

[12] DU K-l. and Swamy M. N. Wireless Communication Systems. New York: Cambridge University Press, 2010.

[13] Cumming I. G. and Wong F. H. Digital Processing of Synthetic Aperture Radar Data. London: Artech House, 2004.

[14] Woo J. C., Lim B. G., and Kim Y. S. Modification of the Recursive Sidelobe Minimization Technique for the Range-Doppler Algorithm of SAR Imaging. *Journal of Electromagnetic Waves and Applications (JEMWA)*, 25, pp.1783-1794, 2011.

[15] Hossain M. A., Elshafiey I., Alkanhal M., and Mabrouk A. Real-time implementation of UWB-OFDM synthetic aperture radar imaging. *IEEE Int. Conf. on Signal and Image Processing Applications (ICSIPA), Kuala lumpur, Malaysia*, pp.450-455, 2011.

[16] Atoche A. C. and Castillo J. V. Dual Super-Systolic Core for Real-Time Reconstructive Algorithms of High-Resolution Radar/SAR Imaging Systems. *Sensors*, 12, pp. 2539-2560, 2012.

Chapter 4

High-Resolution and Hyperspectral Data Fusion for Classification

Hina Pande and Poonam S. Tiwari

Additional information is available at the end of the chapter

http://dx.doi.org/10.5772/56944

1. Introduction

Resolution can be defined as the fineness with which an instrument can distinguish between the different values of some measured attribute. In the context of remotely sensed data references are made to four types of resolutions i.e. spatial resolution, spectral resolution, radiometric resolution and temporal resolution. The spatial resolution refers to the area of smallest resolvable element (e.g. pixel); spectral resolution refers to the smallest wavelength which can be detected in the spectral measurement (Lillesand and Kiefer, 2000). Technically these two types of resolution can be inter-related so that one can be improved at the expense of the others. The information content of an image is based on spatial and spectral resolution of an imaging system. To exploit and explore the benefit of enhanced spatial capability and spectral capability in, fusion techniques were developed to merge complementary information. Fusion of multispectral and panchromatic image has been done in past several times by many researchers for different purposes i.e. for feature extraction, 3D modelling (building extraction etc.). "Image *fusion is the combination of two or more images to form a new image by using a certain algorithm*". (Pohl and Genderen Van, 1998).

"The "hyper" in the hyperspectral means "over" as in "too many" and refers to the large number of measured wavelength bands" (Shippert, 2008). Hyperspectral imaging in remote sensing was a major breakthrough that opened the avenues of research in various fields like mineralogy mapping for oil exploration, environmental geology, vegetation sciences, hydrology, tsunami-aids, biomass estimation and many more due to its ample spectral information contained in hundreds of co-registered bands.

The fusion of hyperspectral with multispectral image results in a new image which has the spatial resolution of the high resolution image and preserves the spectral characteristics of the hyperspectral image. There are some algorithms used specifically to fuse and classify the

Hyperspectral data with the multispectral data. Some of the algorithms are transformation based (e.g. Intensity, Hue, Saturation), wavelet decomposition, neural networks, knowledge-based image fusion, Colour Normalised Transform (CNT), Principal Component Transform (PCT) and the Gram-Schmidt Transform. (Ali Darvishi et al., 2005). Combining hyperspectral and multispectral images can enhance the information content of the image thus help in geospatial data extraction. Fusion of multi-sensor image data has been widely used procedures now-a-days for complementing and enhancing the information content. The present work primarily focuses on the qualitative assessment of the fused image in terms of the spatial and spectral improvement.

The main objective of the present work is the analysis of the high resolution and hyperspectral data fusion using three different approaches (Gram-Schmidt, Principal Component, and Colour Normalised Transform), analyzing the spectral variation due to fusion and its effect on classification and feature extraction.

1.1. Theoretical concepts: Different fusion algorithms

1.1.1. IHS (Intensity Hue Saturation)

According to Chen et al., 2003 in the IHS transformation image fusion, the Intensity (I), the spatial component and the Hue (H) and the Saturation (S), the spectral components of an image are generated from the RGB image. The Intensity (I) component is then substituted by the high resolution panchromatic image to render a new image in RGB, which is referred as the fused image.

1.1.2. Colour Normalised Transform

The Colour Normalised Transform is another fusion technique that uses a mathematical grouping of the colour image and a high resolution image. The Colour Normalised Transform is also named as the Energy Subdivision Transform that employs a high resolution image to sharpen a low resolution image. This algorithm is also called as Brovey Transform. The Brovey Transform algorithm uses a formula that normalises multispectral bands used for a RGB (Red Green Blue) display and multiplies the result by high resolution data to add the intensity or the brightness component of the image. Brovey Transform is used to increase the contrast and intensity in the low and high ends of the histogram and for producing visually appealing images. (Sanjeevi, 2006)

Brovey Transform works as:

$$DN_f = A\,(w_1 * DN_a + w_2 * DN_b) + B$$

$$DN_f = A * DN_a * DN_b + B$$

A and B are scaling and additive factors respectively and w_1 and w_1 weighting parameters. DN_f, DN_a and DN_b refer to digital numbers of the final fused image and the input images a and b respectively.

http://dx.doi.org/10.5772/56944

1.1.3. Wavelets-Transform image fusion

According to Gomez et al., 2001 the wavelet concept is utilized to fuse the two spectral levels of a hyperspectral image with one band of multispectral image. Wavelets generally mean "waves". Image fusion by Wavelet-based method involves two processing steps: first step consists of extracting the details or the structures. The extracted structures are decomposed into three wavelet coefficients based upon the direction that is the vertical, horizontal and the diagonal. Thus, in combining the high resolution image with a low-resolution image, the high-resolution image is first reference stretched three times, each time to match one of the low-resolution band histograms while, the second step necessitates the introduction of these structures/details into each low-resolution image band through the inverse wavelet transform. Thus, the spectral content from the low-resolution band image is preserved because only the scale structures between the two different resolution images are added. (Sanjeevi, 2008)

1.1.4. Gram-Schmidt Transform

Aiazzi et al., 2006 described that the Gram-Schmidt Transform (GST) is another fusion algorithm which is used to fuse a multispectral image with a panchromatic image. The Gram-Schmidt Transform was invented by Brover and Laben in 1998 and patented by Eastman Kodak. This algorithm works in two modes: "mode1" and "mode2". The "mode1" takes the pixel average of the multispectral (MS) bands. The spatial quality in "mode1" is better but suffers from the spectral distortions due to the radiometric difference of the average of the MS bands and the panchromatic image. While, in "mode2" the spectral distortions are not present but suffer from poor enhancement and low sharpness.

1.1.5. Principal Component Transform

The Principal Component Transform (PCT) used to enhance a low resolution image using a high resolution data. The PC band1 is replaced with a high resolution band, which is scaled to match the PC band1. Hence, there is almost no distortion in the spectral information in the fused output image.

The mathematical operation that applies a linear transformation, based on an image-specific matrix is as follows:

$$PC = Wpc * DN$$

Where Wpc = transformation matrix

PC = transformed data (uncorrelated)

DN = original data

2. Literature review

Pohl and Genderen Van, 1998 proposed that image fusion is a tool to combine the multisource imagery using the advanced image processing techniques. According to Pohl and Genderen

Van, 1998, the main objectives of image fusion are to sharpen images, improve geometric corrections, enhance certain features that are not visible in either of the images, replace the defective data, complement the data sets for the improved classification, detect changes using multitemporal data and, substitute the missing information in one of the image with the signals from another source image.

According to Kasetkasem, Arora and Varshney (2004), merging methods are often divided into two categories: first method simultaneously takes into account all bands in the merging process e.g. Hue- Saturation-Value transformation, Principle-Component transformation, Gram-Schmidt transformation technique; the second category deal separately with the spatial information and each spectral band e.g. Brovey transformation, High-Pass-Filter transformation technique.

Ali Darvishi et al., 2005 analysed the capability of the two algorithms that is Gram-Schmidt and the Principal Component transform in the spectral domain. For this purpose two datasets have been taken (Hyperion/ Quickbird-MS and Hyperion/ Spot-Pan). The main objective of the study was the investigation of the two algorithms in the spectral domain and the statistical interpretation of the fused images with the raw Hyperion. The study area was Central Sulawesi in Indonesia. The results of the fusion show that the GST and PCT has almost similar ability in protecting the statistics as compared to the raw Hyperion. The correlation analysis show poor correlation between the raw Hyperion and the fused image bands. The results of the analysis show that the bands located in the high-frequency area of the spectrum better preserve the statistics as compared to the bands located in the low-frequency region. Different statistical parameters like the standard deviation, mean, median, and mode, maximum, minimum values of the raw Hyperion and the two fused images (GST & PCT) were compared for the analysis.

Gomez et al., 2001 has studied the fusion of the hyperspectral data with the multispectral data using the Wavelet-based image fusion. In the present study, two levels of hyperspectral data were used in fusion with one band of multispectral data. The fused image obtained had a RMSE (Root Mean Square Error) of 2.8 per pixel with a SNR (Signal to Noise Ration) of 36 dB. The results show that the fusion of hyperspectral data with the multispectral data produced a composite image of high spatial resolution of the multispectral data with all the spectral characteristics of the hyperspectral data with minimum artifacts. The study concluded that more than two datasets can be fused using the Wavelet transform image fusion technique.

Chen et al., 2003 carried out a study which took the hyperspectral data, AVIRIS (Airborne Visible/ Infrared Imaging Spectrometer) to fuse with TOPSTAR (Topographic Synthetic Aperture Radar) which provides the textural information to get a composite image to study the urban scene. The study has been conducted for the urban area of Park city, Utah. The composite image obtained has been superimposed on the DEM (Digital Elevation Model) generated from the TOPSTAR data to get a 3D perspective. The transformed image obtained was interpreted for the visual discrimination among various urban types. This was possible after fusion of AVIRIS and TOPSTAR data using IHS (Intensity Hue Saturation) transform, which resulted in an image having high spatial and spectral resolution. The objective of the study was to study the areas which are at a risk due to the geological hazards like the avalanches, mudflows etc. The fused image was interpreted for information extraction for assessment and mitigation of these hazards in the area. The results of the fusion of the AVIRIS and TOPSTAR data show better enhancement in the urban features. The spectral resolution of the AVIRIS data helped in better discriminating among various urban features like the buildings and the mining tailings. The MNF-transformed bands of the AVIRIS data also improved the discriminability among the various features. The combined use of the HIS fused data, the MNFtransformed bands and the DEM of the area provided for better understanding of the urban features.

Ling et al., 2006 has analysed the results of fusing the high resolution data like the IKONOS and Quickbird using the Fast Fourier Transform - enhanced IHS method. The study aimed at evaluating the ability of the traditional methods like the HIS and the PCA (Principal Component Analysis) in fusing the high resolution data to preserve the colour and spectral information in the fused product. The study integrated the IHS transform with the FFT filtering of both the panchromatic and the intensity component of the multispectral image. The study has been done using the IKONOS and the Quickbird data. The analysis prove that the HIS transform using the FFT filtering improved the results in preserving the high spatial quality and the spectral characteristics.

3. Data used and study area

3.1. Hyperion

Hyperion is an EO-1 (Earth Observation-1) sensor which was developed under NASA's new millennium program in November, 2000. The level 1 product used in the present study has 242 bands in the range of 355-2577 nm at 10 nm bandwidth (Table 1). Out of these 242 bands only 198 bands are calibrated. The bands which are not calibrated are set to zero.

3.2. IKONOS (MSS & Panchromatic)

IKONOS was the first commercial high resolution satellite to be positioned into the orbit. The IKONOS (MSS) image has 4 bands (red, green, blue, NIR) with 4m spatial resolution and IKONOS (Pan) has one band (.4-.9 μm) with 1m spatial resolution (Table 1).

3.3. Study area

For the present study datasets of two areas were selected- Dehradun and Udaipur city area.

The city of Dehradun is situated in the south central part of Dehradun district. Dehradun city lies at 30°19' N and 78°20' E. The city is located at an altitude of 640 m above MSL. The lowest altitude is 600 m in the southern board is 38.04 sq. Km. The highest altitude is 1000 m in the northern part of the city. The site where the city is located slopes gently from north to south direction. The northern part of the region is heavily dissected by a number of seasonal streams (Fig 1a). The study strip can be divided into two distinct land cover classes:

1. The western portion is dominated with varied vegetation of Sal, Teak, Bamboo, etc.

Sensor Altitude	705Km
Spatial Resolution	30 mt
Radiometric Resolution	16 bit
Swath	7.2 Km
IFOV (mrad)	0.043
No.Of Rows	256
No.of Columns	3128
VNIR Spectral Range	0.45-1.35 μm
SWIR Spectral Range	1.40-2.48 μm
Altitude	681 Km
Inclination	98.2^0
Repeat Cycle	14 day
Sensor	Optical Sensor Assembly
Swath width	11Km
Off Nadir Viewing	+-Omnidirectional
Revisit time	1-3 days
Spatial Resolution	1m (PAN), 4m (MSS)
Spectral Bands (μm)	0.45-0.52 0.52-0.60 0.63-0.69 0.76-0.90 0.45-0.90 (PAN)

Table 1. Technical Specification of the (a) Hyperion and (b)IKONOS (XS and PAN) sensors

2. The southern part with the urban and some patches of vegetation.

The urban pattern in Dehradun city is rather scattered and irregular. The northern part again consists of varied LULC classes like the crop fields, fallow land, urban, grassland, shrubs, and vegetation of mix type. A seasonal river named Tons flows from North East to South West direction. Geomorphically, the northern part of the region is occupied by piedmont fan of post-Siwalik Dun gravels called the Donga fan. Donga fan is a region in the Dehradun city that consists of the varied LULC classes.

Udaipur, Rajasthan, India has been selected as the second study area. Rajasthan is one of the mineral rich states of India. This north-western state of India occupies a place of pride in production and marketing of metallic and non metallic minerals in India. The Aravalli range, one of the oldest mountain ranges of the world runs along the NE–SW direction for more than 720 km, covering nearly 40, 000 km2. The study area (Longitude 73° 32′ 58″ to 73° 49′ 35″ E and Latitude 24° 08′ 18″ to 24° 59′ 53″ N) covers an area of about 750 km2 of this main block of the Aravalli range corresponding to path and row number 146/40 corresponding to full scene of Hyperion (Fig 1 b).

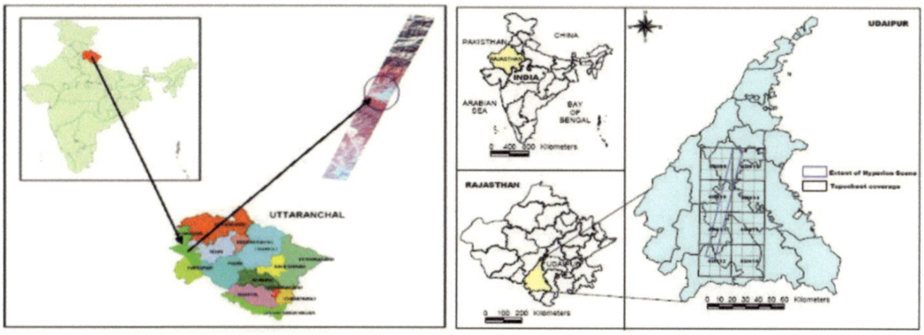

(a) (b)

Figure 1. Study area (a) Dehradun (b) Udaipur

4. Methodology

The methodology adopted was chosen to analyze the performance of the hyperspectral and high-resolution data fusion for classification. The major objective of the study was to comparatively evaluate the three algorithms i.e. the GS (Gram-Schmidt), PC (Principal Component) and the CN (Colour Normalised) Transform on the fusion of Hyperion data with the high-spatial resolution IKONOS (mss) data. The fused images were analysed for pros and cons of the spectral domain image fusion models. For analyzing the spectral variation due to fusion, major land cover areas were identified. The original Hyperion spectra over these landcover areas was compared visually with the fused spectra over same area. The analysis was carried out visually and statistically by comparing spectral profiles of different features with the original Hyperion profiles. (Fig 2).Overall classification accuracy has been used to evaluate the Hyperion data, multispectral IKONOS and the fused data for the two study areas. The methodology is divided in 3 broad steps (Fig 2):

4.1. Pre-processing stage

The Hyperion Level 1R product used was having many bad lines and columns in the different bands. Thus radiometric correction for removal of bad columns was performed by calculating the average of the DN values of the adjacent columns. Atmospheric correction techniques have been developed in order to allow the retrieval of pure ground radiances from the target materials. The haziness in atmosphere accounts for the reduced radiation from Sun reaching the Earth surface causing blurriness in the image. Due to this reason, the atmospheric correction for the Hyperion image was considered important in the present study. In the present work, the FLAASH model in ENVI 4.5 is chosen which is a first-principles atmospheric correction modelling tool for retrieving spectral reflectance from hyperion. The spectral subsets for the Hyperion data have been created in the same wavelength range as that of the IKONOS i.e. 400-900 nm and so band number 12 to 55 are used. So, in total, the Hyperion image file has been reduced from resized 117 bands to 36 bands. Co-registration of hyperion image has been done within IKONOS MSS. The amount of RMS in the registration processes was about 0.823 pixels.

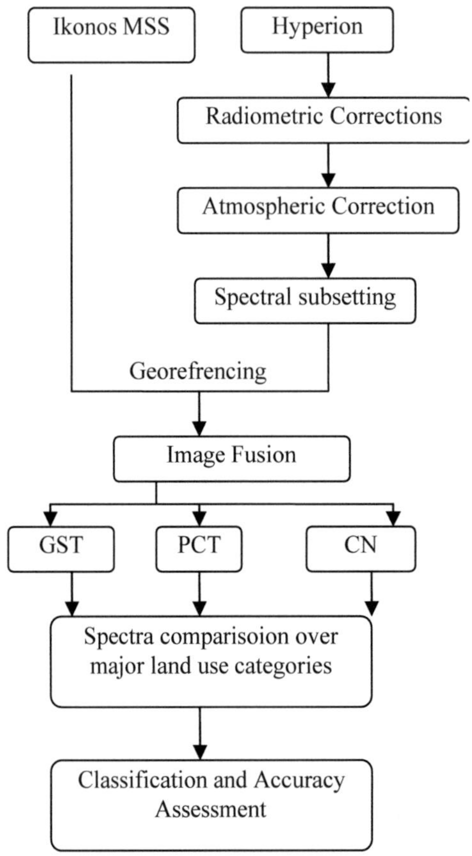

Figure 2. Methodology for comparative evaluation of fusion algorithms on classification accuracy

4.2. Image fusion

Image fusion is the phenomenon of combination of one or more images using an algorithm to acquire a composite image which caters with better and enhanced spatial and spectral information. After developing the spectral subsets for the Hyperion image its individual (R, G, B and NIR) band has been fused with the R, G, B and NIR band of IKONOS data utilizing Principal component Transformation, Gram-Schmidt Transformation (GST) and Color Normalized Transformation. The merging of the spectral subsets of the Hyperion image file (R, G, B and NIR

http://dx.doi.org/10.5772/56944

bands) with the IKONOS (R, G, B and NIR bands) produced four separate. These separate images were then stacked to get one single 36 band image which achieved the spatial resolution of IKONOS and the spectral characteristics of the Hyperion image (Fig 3 & 4).

(a)CN Fused Image (b) PC Fused Image (c)GST Fused Image

Figure 3. Figure 3: Hyperion and IKONOS MSS fused images for part of Dehradun area (a: Fusion using CN Transform, b: Fusion using PC Transform, c: Fusion using GS Transform)

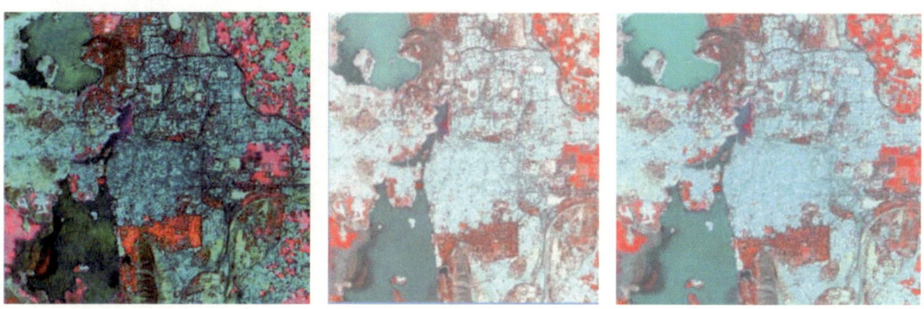

(a)CN Fused Image (b) PC Fused Image (c)GST Fused Image

Figure 4. Hyperion and IKONOS MSS fused images for part of Udaipur area (a: Fusion using CN Transform, b: Fusion using PC Transform, c: Fusion using GS Transform)

4.3. Spectra comparision

The spectral profiles of the various land cover classes present in the scene area like vegetation, bare soil, crop land, fallow land etc. and three fused products have been compared with the Hyperion.

4.3.1. Vegetation

In the Hyperion image, we observe that in the beginning there is a slow rise in the curve starting from the wavelength of 500 nm to a value of more than 250 and there exists a short peak in the blue region. At a wavelength of 700 nm there is a sharp rise in the curve that reaches to a value of 2000 and then there exists some small peaks in the NIR region which establishes that vegetation is best discriminated in this region. In the CN fused image, the outcomes of the spectral profile is almost similar with only one remarkable difference that is in the reflectance value. The vegetation here shows a rise in reflectance value only up to 450-750. In the PC fused image, the results are different with respect to Hyperion and CN fused image. The spectral profile of the GS fused image is almost similar to the PC fused image (Fig 5).

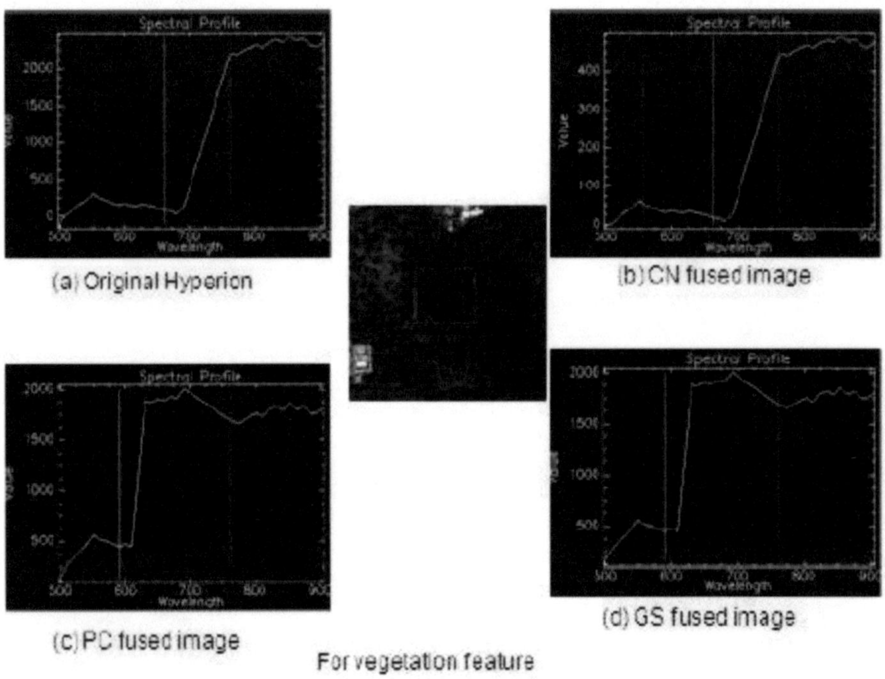

Figure 5. Spectral profiles for Sal Vegetation

4.3.2. Building

In the Hyperion image, the curve starts rising slowly from the blue region up to a value of 1000 and then suddenly at the green edges the slope of the curve increases and there is a linear rise in the curve up to a value of 2500. In the NIR end small peaks are observed. Similar sort of consequences are observed in the CN fused image but the value is limited only up to 800. The results of the PC fused image are somewhat different. The building feature seen above is enhanced with values ranging more than 4000. The rise starts from the blue region that reaches to a peak at 1625. In between green and the red region of the spectrum, the rise is continuous. The curve is flattened at a value of 1500 but suddenly the curve rises at 680 nm with a steep slope that reaches a maximum value of 3900. Then after the red region, small peaks are observed. The spectrum observed for the GS fused image is same as the PC fused image (Fig 6).

http://dx.doi.org/10.5772/56944

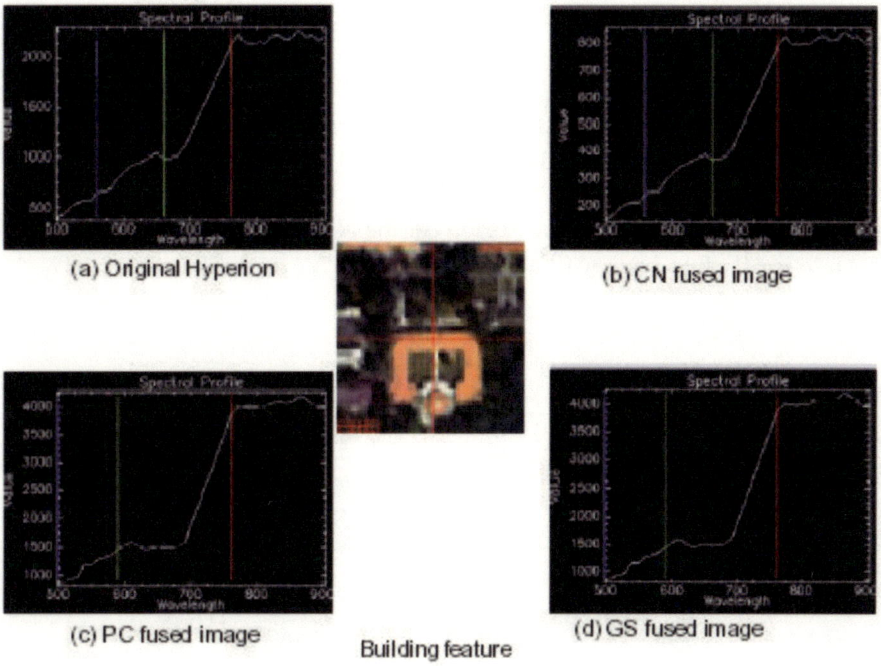

Figure 6. Spectral profiles for Bulding with terracotta roof

4.3.3. Bare soil

The spectral profile of the bare soil shows variations in the Hyperion image. The curve rises with a high slope and one can observe short peaks at wavelengths of 580 nm, 680 nm and highest rise at 820 nm. The rise in the curve is not uniform as there are some dumpy peaks and dips in the curve. Only, between blue and the green region, the rise is somewhat linear with one peak at 580 nm. In between the green and the red region, one enhanced peak can be observed at 680 nm but near to the red region at a value of about 3360 there is a flat dip. In the NIR region, some undulations are present in the curve with a peak at a value of about 3680 at 820 nm. In the CN fused image, one can observe a number of dips and peaks in the curve. The curve initially rises and meets a pointed peak with a value near to 500 at 515 nm. Then, in between the blue and the green region, the curve rises with a steep slope with two peaks at a value of 612.5 and 662.5 at 580 nm and 650 nm. There is a small dip after the green end. In between the green and the red region, there is a peak at a value of about 637.5 at 680 nm. After the rise, there is a flat dip at the red region but after this dip the curve rises again in the NIR region with some flat peaks and a sharp dip at a value of 637.5 at 875 nm wavelength. In the PC and the GS fused image, the range of the reflectance value is from 2000-4500. The spectral profile of the bare soil in the PC fused image shows some remarkable outcomes. The curve first rises slowly till the green end and then there is a sudden and sharp fall in the curve till it reaches a value below 2000 at 630 nm. The dip in the curve remains constant till it reaches 2000 at 690 nm but after that the curve rises sharply with a steep slope till the value of about 4750 at the red end. After the red end, in the NIR region the curve is runs almost flat with a little dip at 4500 at 875 nm. The result of the spectral profile of the bare soil in the GS fused image is almost similar to the profile in the PC fused image with minor differences at certain points. Initially, the curve rises and a small peak is encountered at a value of about 2250 at 520 nm wavelength. The curve rises again in the same way as in the PC fused image. The curve runs almost flat below the value of about 2000 in between 630-695 nm. After this the curve rises sharply with a steep slope till the red region. In the NIR region, the outcomes are almost comparable as the PC fused image (Fig 7).

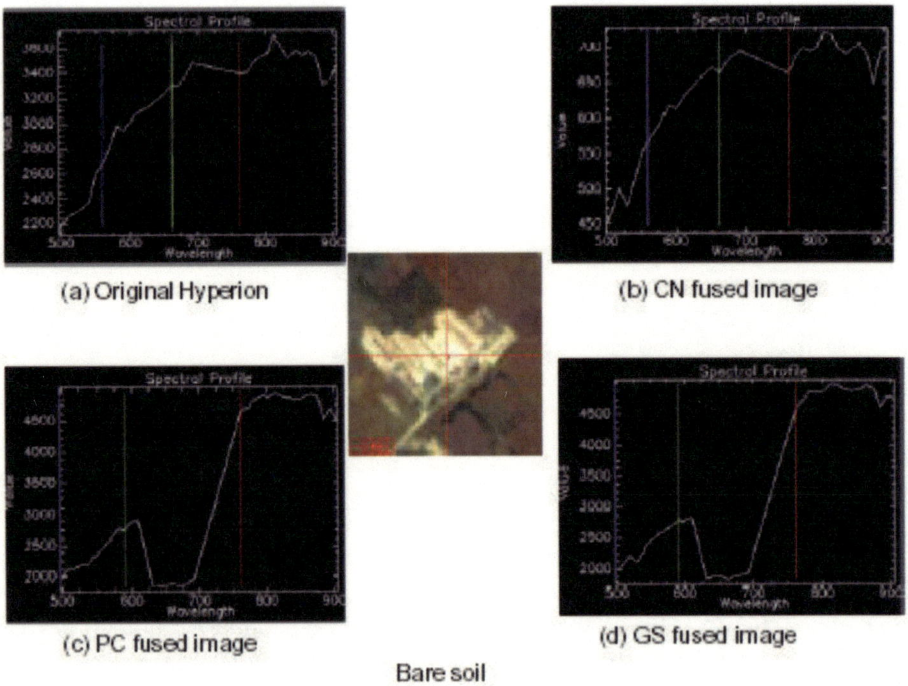

Figure 7. Spectral profiles for Bare soil

4.3.4. Fallow land

In the Hyperion image, we observe a continuous rise in the curve up to a value of 3625. For fallow land, the rise starts from wavelength of 500 nm and the slope of the curve is not that much steep. The rise in the curve is continuous with no noteworthy dips. In the CN fused image, the events are similar to the Hyperion but there is a difference in the range of the reflectance value up to which the curve rises. The range of the values in the CN fused image is limited to 400. In the PC fused image, the curve starts rising from the wavelength of 500 nm up to 750 and then there is a small dip. The dip is not remarkable and then again the curve rises. The curve rises linearly with a steep slope in between green and the red region up to value of 2500 and then again in the NIR region (beyond 750 nm) small pronounced peaks are present. The spectral profile of the fallow land in the GS fused image is almost comparable in the PC fused image (Fig 8).

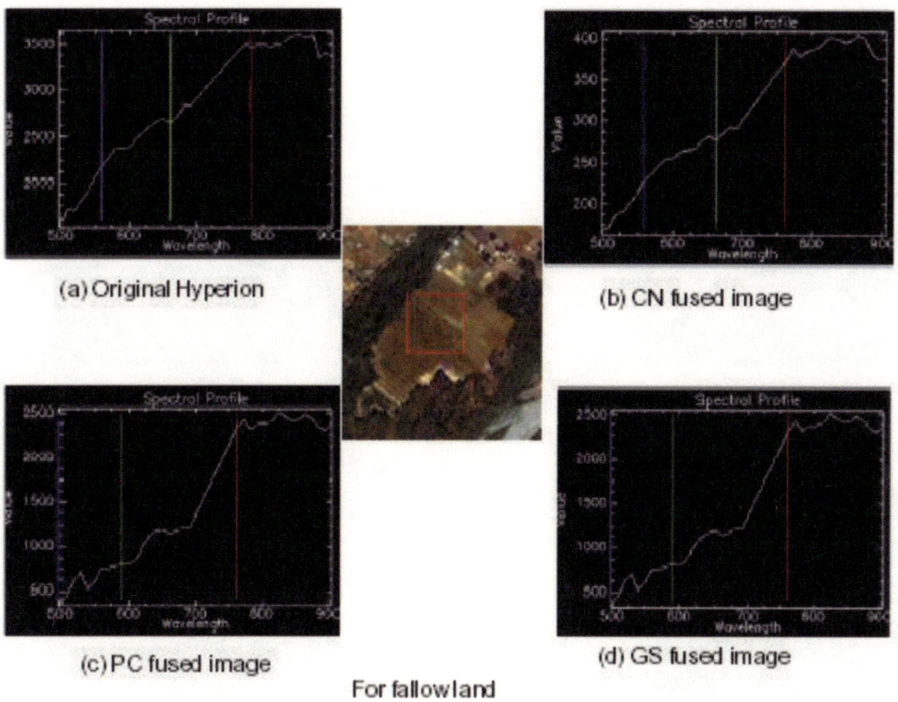

Figure 8. Spectral profiles for Fallow Land

4.3.5. Dry river

The spectral profile of river in the Hyperion image show lots of undulations i.e. a number of peaks and dips are observed. The curve rises sharply until it reaches a value of about 1820 at 520 nm. At 520 nm there is a pointed peak and then there is a small dip at about 530 nm. Again, the curve rises till it reaches a value of about 2050 at 590 nm. Then, suddenly the curve falls down till it reaches a value of about 1900 at 665 nm. After the fall in the curve, the curve again starts rising till it reach the red end. In the NIR region, the curve consists of two pointed peaks at 775 nm and 600 nm. After this the curve again drops to a value of about 1965 at 890 nm. In the CN fused image, the curve rises gently up to low values. There is a flattened peak at the blue region and then after the blue region the curve drops down almost flat till 690 nm. After

690 nm the curve rises sharply till the red region is encountered at 660 nm. In the NIR region, the curve runs almost flat with wide contiguous bands. In the PC fused image, the curve starts at the value of about 1500 in the blue region. The curve runs parallel to the ground till the value of about 1750 at 620 nm. After this the curve suddenly drops down and the dip encountered in the region between the blue and the red end is almost flat. At 690 nm, suddenly there is a steep rise in the curve till it reaches a value of about 3375 at 775 nm. After this in the NIR region, the curve again runs flat with small flattened peaks. The spectral profile of river in the GS fused image is almost similar to the profile in the PC fused image (Fig 9).

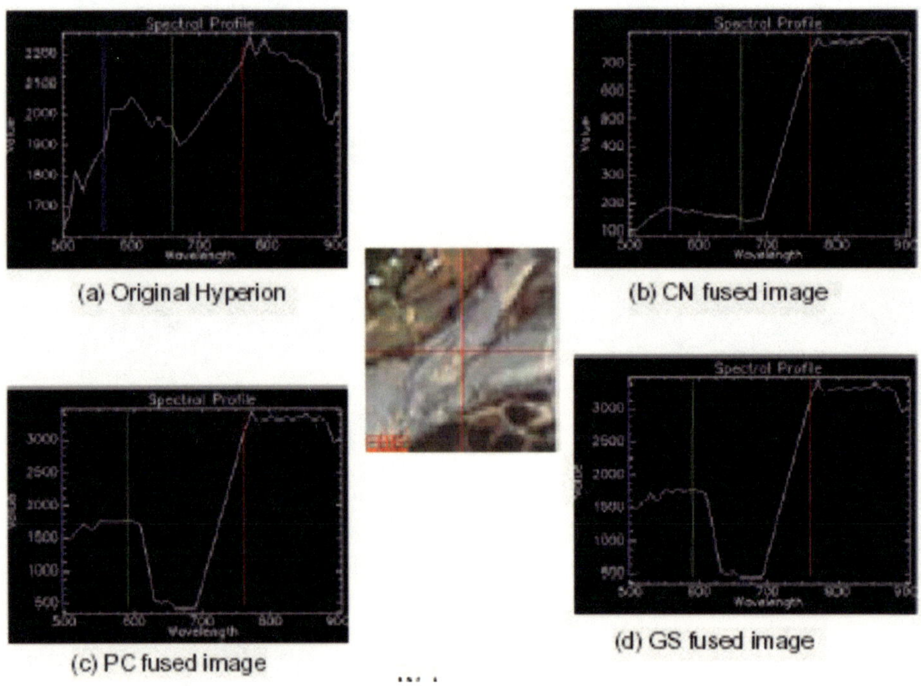

Figure 9. Spectral profiles for Dry River Bed

4.3.6. Land with grass

In the Hyperion image, the curve rises slowly with almost flattened slope till it reaches a value of 1500 at a wavelength of 700 nm but then after that the curve rises linearly with a steep slope. This slope is between green and the red region. At the red region, this sharp rise in the curve is slowed down and then after that in the NIR region the curve rises slowly with one enhanced peak at 4500 at a wavelength of 875 nm. In the CN fused image, the curve rises slowly with a stumpy slope till it reaches 475 at a wavelength of 775 nm till the red region of the spectrum. In the NIR region, we observe some peaks in the curve. In the PC fused image, the curve shows some dips. Initially, the curve rises slowly till 1350 at a wavelength of 610 nm (approximated) then after the green end, the curve shows some variations. After the green end, the curve rises suddenly with a high slope till it reaches a value of 2750 at a wavelength of 680 nm. After 680 nm, the curve shows a decrease in the values till it reaches 2375 at the red region. In the NIR region, again the curve rises with some small peaks. The spectral profile of the grounds with grass in the GS fused image show almost the same outcomes as the PC fused image (Fig 10).

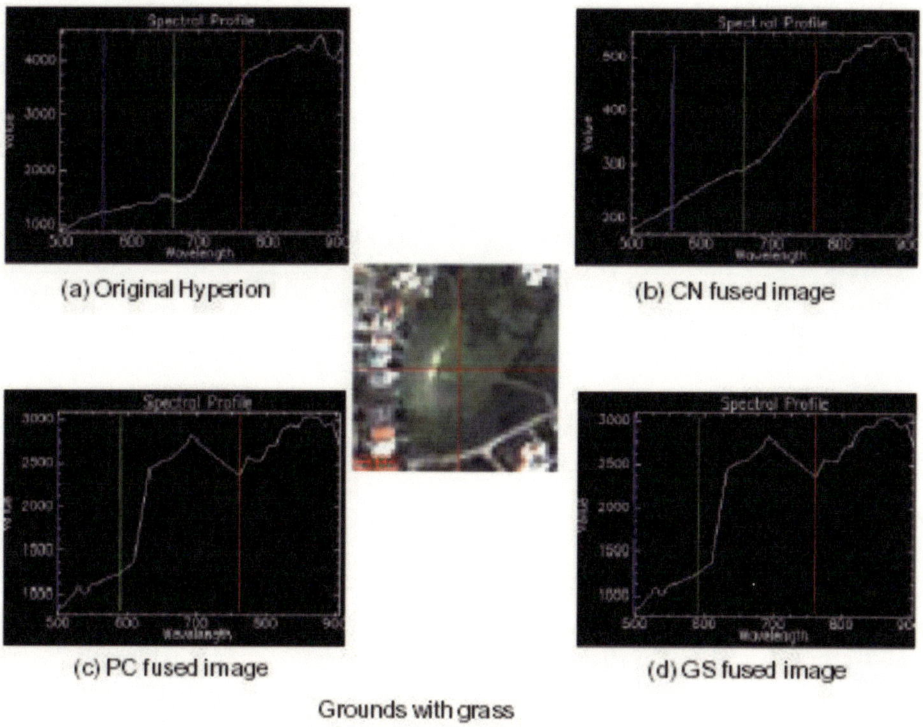

Figure 10. Spectral profiles for Ground with grass

4.4. Classification

In the context of the present work, the original and the three fused datasets were classified by SAM (Spectral Angle Mapper) method of supervised classification. The Spectral Angle Mapper Classification (SAM) is an automated method for directly comparing image spectra to a reference or an endmember. This method treats both spectra as vectors and calculates the spectral angle between them. This method is insensitive to illumination since the SAM algorithm uses only the vector direction and not the vector length. The result of the SAM classification is an image showing the best match at each pixel. The selection of the classification algorithm was also based on the characteristics of the image and the training data. The SAM decision rule of classification classified the image into 9 classes i.e. vegetation type1, vegetation type 2, river, shrubs, urban features, grassland, fallow land, bare soil, and crops.

After the classification was performed the classification accuracy has been computed for the IKONOS, Hyperion and the three merged images (Fig 11 & 12). Samples of each of the class from different locations in the Dehradun and Udaipur city have been collected for accuracy assessment.

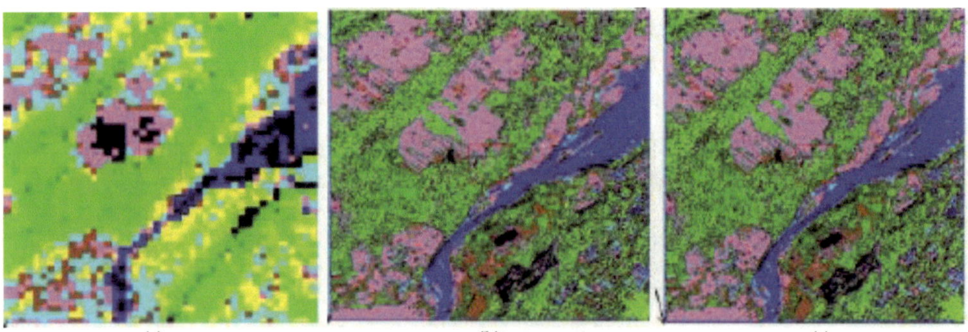

(a) (b) (c)

Figure 11. Classified Product for Hyperion and IKONOS MSS fused images for part of Dehradun area (a: Fusion using CN T, b: Fusion using PC T, c: Fusion using GS T)

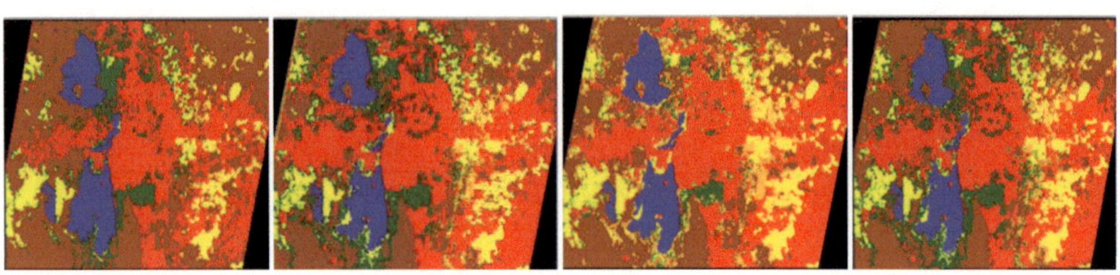

Hyperion Classified CN Fused Classified GST Fused Classified PCT Fused Classified

Figure 12. Classified images (Udaipur)

5. Results and discussions

Although many studies focus on the development of fusion techniques, fewer studies concentrate on the development of image assessment methods. This study concentrates on statistical measures and classification accuracy for fusion performance. Statistical evaluation procedures have the advantage that they are objective, quantitative, and repeatable. The

http://dx.doi.org/10.5772/56944

correlation coefficients between the original hyperion bands and the equivalent fused bands and the other three parameters ie Mean, Standard Deviation, and Median were calculated.

The statistical parameters for various fused products were plotted along with the raw Hyperion image. The graph depicts that there is no noticeable change in the statistics in the original Hyperion and fused products. PCT fused and the GST fused images demonstrate some comparable values for the mean, maximum, minimum and standard deviation but roughly have the same ability in preserving the statistics. The CNT fused image show very low values than the raw Hyperion image (Fig 13 a & b).

After evaluating the spectral profiles we observe that although the range of values in the CN fused image is not comparable to the Hyperion but in most of the cases the shape of the profile closely matches with the profile of the feature in Hyperion. So, we can infer that spectrally the CN (Colour Normalised) approach better preserves the spectral characteristics in the fused image. In terms of the visual discreteness or the spatial characteristics of the various LULC classes in the fused images, GS (Gram-Schmidt) and the PC (Principal Component) transform are best suitable if compared to Hyperion while if compared to IKONOS there is almost no gain in the spatial quality.

For performance analysis of fusion the classified images were analyzed using reference data form ground. The results of classification of the PCT and GST fused image are almost similar though for CN fused image results are deteriorated because of the artificial pixels that hinder in the classification process (Fig 11 & 12). The overall classification accuracy was calculated for the IKONOS, Hyperion and the three merged products. It was observed that the accuracy is improving in PCT fused image and GST fused image while deteriorating in CNT fused Image (Table 2).

The comparison of the separability analysis done to the original data sets and the three fused products, show that the separability for some of the classes increases after fusion and hence the classification accuracy achieved is higher (Fig 14). The classified images show some black pixels not belonging to any of the specified classes. Such pixels are left unclassified as they did not match with the pixel spectrum of any of the land cover class specified, or they are exhibiting a large angular difference (greater than.1 radians) between the known and the unknown pixel spectrum.

Data Product	Overall Accuracy Achieved (Dehradun)	Overall Accuracy Achieved (Udaipur)
IKONOS	75.86%	79.72%
HYPERION	68.15%	63.14%
PCT FUSED IMAGE	80.23%	83.34%
GST FUSED IMAGE	81.12%	80.23%
CNT FUSED IMAGE	65.14%	68.57%

Table 2. Classification Accuracy

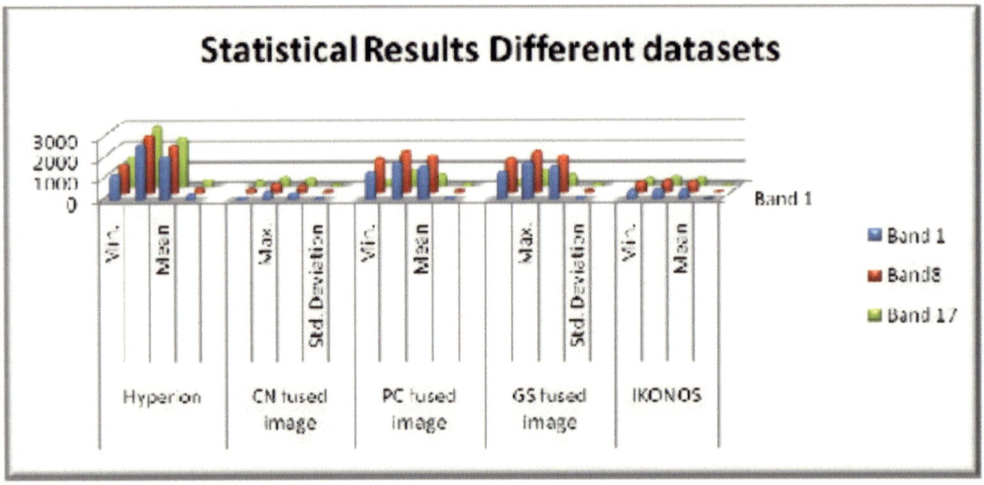

(a)

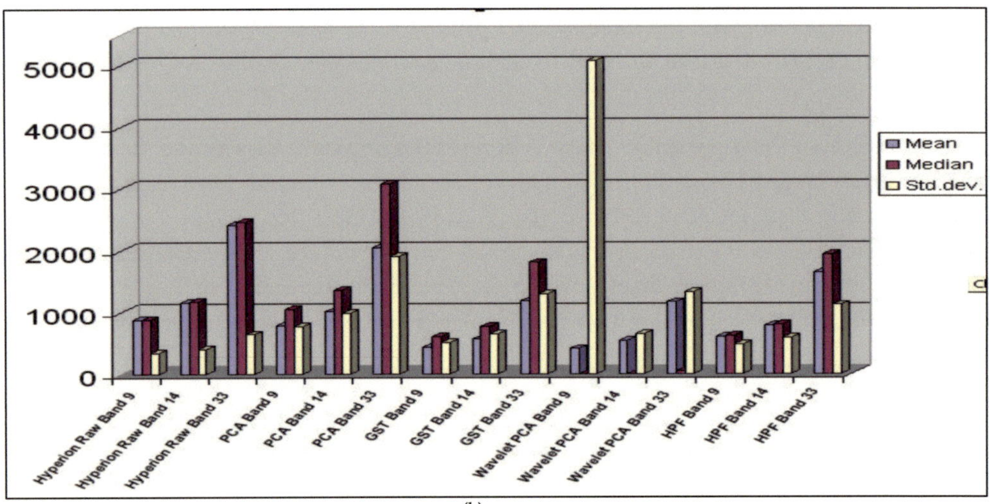

(b)

Figure 13. (a & b): Statistical Comparision of fused images (a: Dehradun, b: Udaipur)

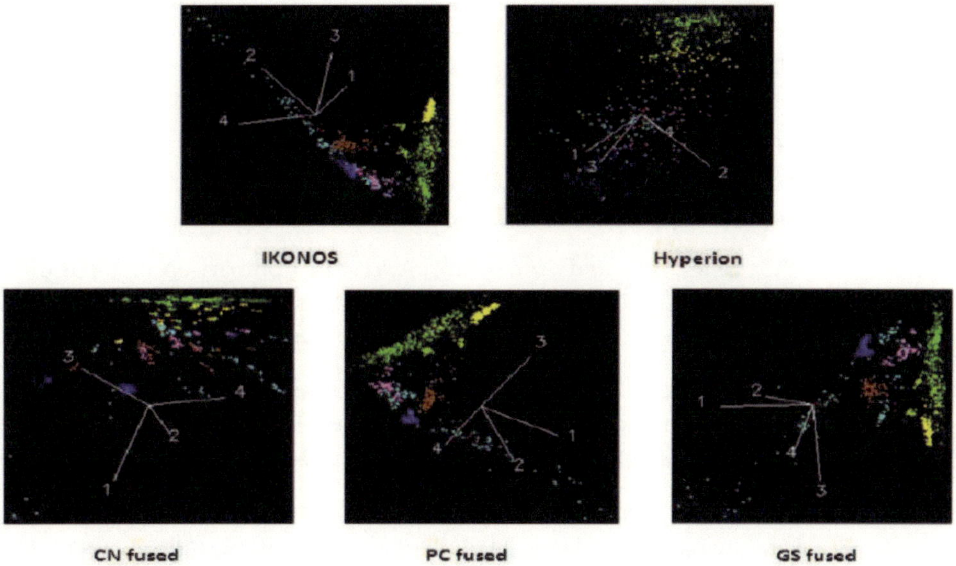

Figure 14. Class seperability analysis for original and Fused images

Author details

Hina Pande* and Poonam S. Tiwari

*Address all correspondence to: hina@iirs.gov.in

Indian Institute of Remote Sensing (ISRO), Dehradun, India

References

[1] Aarthy, R.S. and Sanjeevi, S., 2007. Spectral studies of lunar equivalent rocks-A prelude to lunar mineral mapping. Indian society of Remote Sensing, 35 (2): 141- 152.

[2] Aiazzi, B., Alparone, L., Baronti, S. and Selva, M., 2006. MS + Pan Image Fusion by an Enhanced Gram-Schmidt Spectral Sharpening, Italy. www.igik.edu.pl/earsel2006/abstracts/data_fusion/aiazzi_baronti.pdf (Last Accessed on Nov., 2007)

[3] Ali Darvishi, B., Kuppas, M. and Erasmi, S., 2005. Hyper-spectral/High resolution Data fusion: Assessing the quality of EO1 - Hyperion/spot-Pan and Quickbird-MS fused Images in spectral Domain

[4] Ali Darvishi, B., Kuppas, M. and Erasmi, S., 2005. Hyper-spectral/High resolution Data fusion: Assessing the quality of EO1 - Hyperion/spot-Pan and Quickbird-MS fused Images in spectral Domain. (http://www.ipi.uni-hannover.de/fileadmin/institut/pdf/073-darvishi.pdf)

[5] Alparone L., Baronti S., Garzelli A., Nencini F. (2004), Landsat ETM+ and SAR Image Fusion Based on Generalized Intensity Modulation, IEEE Transactions on Geoscience and Remote Sensing, Vol. 42, No. 12, pp. 2832-2839

[6] Chavez, P.S., Sides, S.C. and Anderson, J.A. (1991): Comparison of three different methods to merge multi-resolution and multi-spectral data: Landsat TM and SPOT Panchromatic, Photogrammetric Engineering and Remote Sensing, 57 (3): 295-303.

[7] Chen, C.-M., Hepner, G.F. and Forster, R.R., 2003. Fusion of Hyperspectral and radar data using the HIS transformation to enhance urban surface features. ISPRS Journal of Photogrammetry and Remote Sensing, 58 (2003): 19-30.

[8] Gomez, B.R., Jazaeri, A. and Kafatos, M., 2001. Wavelet-based hyperspectral and multispectral image fusion. www.scs.gmu.edu/~rgomez/fall01/fusionpaper.pdf (Last Accessed on Nov., 2007)

[9] Kasetkasem, T., Arora, M. K., and Varshney, P. K., "An MRF Model Based Approach for Sub-pixel Mapping from Hyperspectral Data, " Advanced Image Processing Techniques for Remotely Sensed Hyperspectral Data, ed. P. K. Varshney and M. K. Arora, Chapter 11, pp. 279-307, Springer Verlag, 2004.

[10] Li J., Luo J., Ming D., Shen Z. (2005), A New Method for Merging IKONOS Panchromatic and Multispectral Image Data, Geoscience and Remote Sensing Symposium IGARSS, Vol. 6, pp. 3916-3919

[11] Lillesand, M.T. and Kiefer, W.R., 2000. Remote sensing and image interpretation. John Wiley and sons, New york.

[12] Ling, Y., Ehlers, M., Usery, l.E. and Marguerite, M., 2006. FFT-enhanced IHS transform method for fusing high-resolution satellite images. ISPRS Journal of photogrammetry and Remote Sensing, 61 (2007): 381-392.

[13] Photogrammetric Engineering and Remote Sensing, Vol. 57, No.3, pp. 295–303. Photogrammetry & Remote Sensing, Vol. 58, pp. 19-30

[14] Pohl C., Van Genderen J. L. (1998), Multisensor image fusion in remote sensing: Concepts, methods and applications (Review article), International Journal of Remote Sensing, Vol. 19, No. 5, pp. 823-854

[15] Sanjeevi, S., 2006.Chapter on Multisensor Image Fusion. Lecture notes on Advanced Image Processing . Photogrammetry and remote sensing Division Indian institute of remote sensing, Dehradun

http://dx.doi.org/10.5772/56944

[16] Sanjeevi, S., 2008. Chapter on Multisensor Image Fusion. Lecture notes on Advanced Image Processing . Photogrammetry and remote sensing Division Indian institute of remote sensing, Dehradun

[17] Shippert, P., 2008. Introduction to Hyperspectral Image Analysis. http://satjournal.tcom.ohiou.edu/pdf/shippert.pdf (Last Accessed on Nov., 2007)

Chapter 5

The Objective Evaluation Index (OEI) for Evaluation of Night Vision Colorization Techniques

Yufeng Zheng, Wenjie Dong, Genshe Chen and
Erik P. Blasch

Additional information is available at the end of the chapter

http://dx.doi.org/10.5772/56948

1. Introduction

A *night vision colorization* technique can produce colorized imagery with a naturalistic and stable color appearance by processing multispectral night vision (NV) imagery. The multispectral images typically include visual-band (e.g., red, green, and blue (RGB), or intensified) imagery and infrared imagery (e.g., near infrared (NIR) and long wave infrared (LWIR)). Although appropriately false-colored imagery is often helpful for human observers in improving their performance on scene classification and reaction time tasks (Waxman *et al.*, 1996; Essock *et al.*, 1999), inappropriate color mappings can also be detrimental to human performance (Toet et al., 2001; Varga, 1999). A possible reason is lack of physical color constancy. Another drawback with false coloring is that observers need specific training with each of the false color schemes so that they can correctly and quickly recognize objects; whereas with colorized nighttime imagery rendered with natural colors, users should be able to readily recognize and identify objects without any training.

There are several night vision (NV) colorization techniques developed in past decades. Toet (2003) proposed a NV colorization method that transfers the color characteristics of daylight imagery into multispectral NV images. Essentially, this color-mapping method matches the statistical properties (i.e., mean and standard deviation) of the NV imagery to that of a natural daylight color image (manually selected as the "target" color distribution). Zheng and Essock (2008) presented a "local coloring" method that can colorize the NV images more like daylight imagery by using histogram matching. The local-coloring method renders the multispectral images with natural colors segment by segment (i.e., "segmentation-based"), and also provides automatic association between the source and target images. Zheng (2011) recently introduced a *channel-based color fusion* method, which is fast enough for real-time applications. Note that the term "color fusion" in this chapter refers to combing multispectral images into a color-version image with the purpose of resembling natural scenes. Hogervorst and Toet (2008 & 2012) recently proposed a new color mapping method using a lookup table (LUT). The LUT is created between a false-colored image (formed with multispectral NV images) and its color reference image (aiming at the same scene but taken at daytime). The colors in the resulting colored NV image resemble the colors in the daytime color image. This LUT-mapping method runs fast for real-time implementations. The LUT-mapping method and the statistic-matching method are also summarized in their recent paper (Toet & Hogervorst, 2012). Most recently Zheng (2012) developed a joint-histogram matching method for NV colorization.

The quality of colorized images can be assessed by subjective and/or objective measures. However, subjective evaluation normally costs time and resources. Moreover, the subjective evaluation methods cannot be readily and routinely used for real-time and automated systems. On the other hand, objective evaluation metrics can automatically and quantitatively measure the image qualities (Liu *et al.*, 2012 & Blasch *et al.*, 2008). Over the past decade, many objective metrics for grayscale image evaluations have been proposed (Alparone *et al.*, 2004; Wald *et al.*, 1997; Tsagaris & Anastassopoulos, 2006). However, the metrics for grayscale images cannot be directly extended to the evaluations of colorized images. Recently, some objective evaluations of color images have been reported in the literature. To objectively assess a color fusion method, Tsagaris (2009) proposed a color image fusion measure (CIFM) by using the amount of common information between the source images and the colorized image, and also the distribution of color information. Yuan *et al.* (2011) presented an objective evaluation method for visible and infrared color fusion utilizing four metrics: image sharpness metric, image contrast metric, color colorfulness metric, and color naturalness metric. In this chapter, we introduce an *objective evaluation index* (OEI) to quantitatively evaluate the colorized images. Given a reference (daylight color) image and several versions of the colorized NV images from different coloring techniques, all color images are first converted into International Commission on Illumination (CIE) LAB space, with dimension $\boldsymbol{L}$ for lightness and $\boldsymbol{a}$ and $\boldsymbol{b}$ for the color-opponent dimensions (Malacara, 2002). Then the OEI metric is computed with the four established metrics, phase congruency metric (PCM), gradient magnitude metric (GMM), image contrast metric (ICM), and color natural metric (CNM).

Certainly, a color presentation of multispectral night vision images can provide a better visual result for human users. We would prefer the color images resembling natural daylight pictures that we are used to; meanwhile the coloring process shall be efficient enough ideally for real time applications. In this chapter, we will discuss and explore how to objectively evaluate the image qualities of colorized images. The remainder of this chapter is organized as follows. Six NV colorization techniques are briefly reviewed in Section 2. Next, four image quality metrics are described in Section 3. A new colorization metric, *objective evaluation index* (OEI), is introduced in Section 4. The experiments and discussions are presented in Section 5. Conclusions are finally drawn in Section 6.

2. Overview of night vision colorization techniques

All color mapping methods described in Subsections 2.2-2.6 are performed in *lαβ* color space. Thus the color space conversion from RGB to *lαβ* must be done prior to color mapping, and then the inverse transformation to RGB space is necessary after the mapping. The details of *lαβ* color space transformation are given elsewhere (Toet, 2003; Zheng & Essock, 2008). Certainly, two images, a *source* image and a *target* image, are involved in a color mapping process. The source image is usually a color fusion image (in Subsections 2.2-2.5) or a false-colored image (in Subsection 2.6); while the target image is normally a daylight picture containing the similar scene. The target image may have a different resolution as depicted in Subsections 2.2-2.5; however, the LUT described in Subsection 2.6 is established using the registered target (reference) image.

2.1. Channel-based color fusion (CBCF)

A fast color fusion method, termed as *channel-based color fusion* (CBCF), was introduced to facilitate realtime applications (Zheng, 2011). Notice that the term of "color fusion" means combing multispectral images into a color-version image with the purpose of resembling natural scenes. Relative to the "segmentation-based colorization" (Zheng & Essock, 2008), color fusion trades the realism of colors with speed.

The general framework of channel-based color fusion is as follows, (i) prepare for color fusion, preprocessing (denoising, normalization and enhancement) and image registration; (ii) form a color fusion image by properly assigning multispectral images to red, green, and blue channels; (iii) then fuse multispectral images (gray fusion) using *a*DWT algorithm (Zheng *et al.*, 2005); and, (iv) replace the *value* component of color fusion in HSV color space with the gray-fusion image, and finally transform back to RGB space.

In NV imaging, there may be several bands of images available, for example, visible (RGB), image intensified (II), near infrared (NIR), medium wave infrared (MWIR), long wave infrared (LWIR). Upon the available images and the context, we only discuss two of two-band color fusions of (II ⊕ LWIR), (NIR ⊕ LWIR). The symbol '⊕' denotes the fusion of multiband images.

A color fusion of NIR and LWIR is formulated by,

$$\begin{aligned} &F_R = S_{[0,1.0]}^{[0.2,0.9]}\left(I_{LWIR}\right), && \text{(a)} \\ &F_G = S_{[0.1,I\_Gmax]}^{[0.2,1]}\left(I_{NIR}\right), && \text{(b)} \\ &F_B = S_{[0,1.0]}^{[0.1,0.7]}\left(\left[1.0\text{-}\ I_{LWIR}\right]\bullet I_{NIR}\right); && \text{(c)} \\ &V_F = Fus\left(I_{NIR}, I_{LWIR}\right); && \text{(d)} \end{aligned} \tag{1}$$

where $S_{[0.1,I\_Gmax]}^{[0.2,1]}$ denotes *piecewise contrast stretching* defined in Eq. (2) and $I_{\_Gmax}$ = $min([\mu_{NIR} + 2\sigma_{NIR}], 0.8)$, *min*() is an operation to get the minimal number; [1.0- I_{LWIR}] is to invert

LWIR image; symbol '•' means element-by-element multiplication; V_F is the *value* component of F_C in HSV space, *Fus*() means image fusion operation using *a*DWT algorithm (Zheng *et al.*, 2005). Although the limits given in contrast stretching are obtained empirically according to the night vision images that we had, it is viable to formulate the expressions and automate the fusion based upon a set of conditions (imaging devices, imaging time, and application location). Notice the transform parameters in Eqs. (1) were applied to all color fusions in our experiments (see Fig. 3d).

$$\mathbf{I}_S = S_{[I_{Min}, I_{Max}]}^{[L_{Min}, L_{Max}]} = (\mathbf{I}_0 - I_{\text{Min}})\frac{L_{\text{Max}} - L_{\text{Min}}}{I_{\text{Max}} - I_{\text{Min}}} + L_{\text{Min}}, \tag{2}$$

where $\mathbf{I}_S$ is the scaled image, $\mathbf{I}_0$ is the original image; I_{Min} and I_{Max} are the maximum and minimum pixel values in $\mathbf{I}_0$, respectively; L_{Min} and L_{Max} are the expected minimum and maximum pixel values in $\mathbf{I}_S$, respectively. After the image contrast stretching, $\mathbf{I}_S \in [L_{\text{Min}}, L_{\text{Max}}]$.

2.2. Statistic matching

A *statistic matching* (stat-match) is used to transfer the color characteristics from natural daylight imagery to false color night-vision imagery, which is formulated as:

$$I_C^k = (I_S^k - \mu_S^k) \cdot \frac{\sigma_T^k}{\sigma_S^k} + \mu_T^k, \text{ for } k = \left\{l, \alpha, \beta\right\}, \tag{3}$$

where I_C is the colored image, I_S is the source (false-color) image in $l\alpha\beta$ space; μ denotes the mean and σ denotes the standard deviation; the subscripts 'S' and 'T' refer to the source and target images, respectively; and the superscript 'k' is one of the color components: $\{l, \alpha, \beta\}$.

After this transformation, the pixels comprising the multispectral source image have means and standard deviations that conform to the target daylight color picture in $l\alpha\beta$ space. The colored image is transformed back to the RGB space through the inverse transforms (Zheng & Essock, 2008; see Fig. 3e).

2.3. Histogram matching (HM)

Histogram matching (i.e., histogram specification) is usually used to enhance an image when histogram equalization fails (Gonzalez & Woods, 2002). Given the shape of the histogram that we want the enhanced image to have, histogram matching can generate a processed (i.e., matched) image that has the specified histogram. In particular, by specifying the histogram of a target image (with daylight natural colors), a source image (with false colors) resembles the target image in terms of histogram distribution after histogram matching.

Histogram matching (hist-match) can be implemented as follows. First, the *normalized cumulative histograms* of source image and target image (h_S and h_T) are calculated, respectively.

$$h_S = S(u_k) = (L-1) \cdot \sum_{0}^{L-1} \frac{n_k}{N}, \tag{4}$$

where N is the total number of pixels in the image, n_k is the number of pixels that have gray level u_k, and L is the number of gray (bin) levels in the image. Typically, $L = 256$ for a digital image. But we can round the image down to m ($m < L$, e.g., $m = 64$) levels, and thus its histogram is called m-bin histogram. Clearly, $S(u_k)$ is a non-decreasing function. Similarly, $h_T = T(v_k)$ can be computed (see the "Target" curve in Fig. 1c).

Second, considering $h_S = h_T$ (i.e., $S(u_k) = T(v_k)$) for histogram matching, the matched image is accordingly computed as

$$v_k = T^{-1}[S(u_k)],\ k = 0,1,2,\ldots,L-1. \tag{5}$$

It is straightforward to find a discrete solution of the inverse transform, $T^{-1}[S()]$ as both $T()$ and $S()$ can be implemented with look up tables.

Similar to the statistic matching (described in Subsection 2.2), histogram matching also serves for color mapping (see Fig. 3f) and is performed component-by-component in $l\alpha\beta$ space. Specifically, with each color component (say the α component, treated as a grayscale image) of a false-colored image, we can compute $S(u_k)$. With a selected target image, $T(v_k)$ can be calculated with regard to the same color component (say α). Using Eq. (5) the histogram matching can be completed regarding the color component (α). Histogram matching and statistic matching can be applied separately or jointly. When applied together, for instance, it is referred to as "statistic matching then histogram matching" (Zheng & Essock, 2008).

2.4. Joint histogram matching (JHM)

As described in Subsection 2.3, histogram matching is applied to each color component (plane) separately. It is highly possible to distort the color distributions of the mapped image (see Fig. 3f). To avoid color distortion, we introduce a new color mapping method, joint histogram matching (joint-HM).

In $l\alpha\beta$ space, α and β represent the color distributions; while l is the intensity component. A *joint histogram* (also called 2D histogram) of two color planes (α versus β) is calculated and then matched from source to target. The intensity component (l) is matched individually. The joint histogram is actually the joint (2D) intensity distribution of the two images, which is often used to compute the joint entropy (Hill & Batchelor, 2001) for image registration.

How to calculate the normalized cumulative histogram (denoted as h) from a 2D joint histogram (denoted as H_J) needs further discussion. To do histogram matching, h is expected to be a non-decreasing function. We propose to form a one-dimensional (1D) histogram by stacking H_J column-by-column and then perform histogram matching as defined in Eq. (10). Of course, to correctly index a 1D transform ($T^{-1}()$), the proper calculation of u_m (with m bins) using two gray (bin) levels is expected. If H_J is computed as (β vs. α), its matching process is denoted as joint-HM($\beta\alpha$). Eventually, the histogram of the mapped image is sort of tradeoff between two histograms, "Source" and "Target". This is expected since we want no color distortion (i.e., preserving its own colors to some extent) during color mapping (see Fig. 3g).

2.5. Statistic matching then joint-histogram matching (SM-JHM)

The joint-HM can be applied together with statistic matching such as "stat-match then joint-HM", which usually result a better NV colorization. The statistic matching globally "paints" the image, while the joint-HM colors is more like the daylight picture in details (see Fig. 3h).

2.6. Lookup table (LUT)

Hogervorst and Toet (2008) proposed a color mapping method using a lookup table (LUT). The LUT is created using a false-colored image (formed with two-band NV images) and the reference (i.e., target) daylight image. This method yields a colored NV image similar to the daytime image in colors. The implementation of this LUT method is described as follows.

1. Create a false-colored image (of 3 color planes) by assigning LWIR image to R, NIR image to G plane, and zeros to B, respectively;
2. Build RG colormap (i.e., a 256×256 LUT) and convert the false-colored image to an indexed image (0 to 65535) associated with the RG colormap;
3. For all pixels in the indexed false-colored image whose index value equals 0:
   a. Locate all corresponding pixels in the reference (i.e., target) color image (that must be strictly aligned with the false-colored image);
   b. Calculate the averaged $l\alpha\beta$ values of those corresponding pixels and then convert them back to RGB values;
   c. Assign the RGB values to *index 0* in the lookup table;
4. Vary the index value from 2 to 65535 and repeat the processes described in Step 3. At the end, the LUT will be established.

Once the LUT is created, the LUT-based mapping procedure is simple and fast (see Fig. 3i), and thus can be deployed in realtime. However, the LUT creation thoroughly relies on the aligned reference image aiming at the same scene. Any misalignment, using a different reference color image, or coloring a different NV imagery (i.e., aiming at different direction), will usually result a poor colorization (see Fig. 5i).

3. Four image quality metrics

Three image quality metrics for grayscale images and one metric for color images are reviewed in this section. The color-related metrics are defined in the CIELAB space (Malacara, 2002) specified by the International Commission on Illumination. The perceptually uniform CIELAB space consists of an achromatic luminosity component L^* (black-white) and two chromatic values a^* (green-magenta) and b^* (blue-yellow). The coordinates $L^*a^*b^*$ (CIE 1976) can be calculated using the CIE XYZ tristimulus values (Malacara, 2002).

3.1. Phase Congruency Metric (PCM)

The *phase congruency* (PC) model is also called the "local energy model" developed by Morrone *et al.* (1986). This model postulates that the features in an image are perceived at the points where the Fourier components are maximal in phase. Based on the physiological and psychophysical evidences, the PC theory provides a simple but biologically plausible model of how mammalian visual systems detect and identify the features in an image. PC can be considered as a significance measure of local structures in an image.

According to the definition of PC (Morrone *et al.*, 1986), there are many different implementations of PC map developed so far. A widely-used method developed by Kovesi (1999) is adopted in this chapter. Given a 1D image $f(x)$, M_n^e and M_n^o represent the even-symmetric and odd-symmetric filters at scale n, respectively. M_n^e and M_n^o form a quadrature pair: $e_n(x)$ and $o_n(x)$. Responses of the quadrature pair form a response vector:

$$\begin{bmatrix} e_n(x) \\ o_n(x) \end{bmatrix} = \begin{bmatrix} f(x) * M_n^e \\ f(x) * M_n^o \end{bmatrix}, \tag{6}$$

and the local amplitude at scale n is

$$A_n(x) = \sqrt{e_n^2(x) + o_n^2(x)}. \tag{7}$$

Let

$$F(x) = \sum_n e_n(x), \; H(x) = \sum_n o_n(x). \tag{8}$$

The one-dimensional (1D) *phase congruency metric* (PCM) can be computed as

$$PC(x) = \frac{\sqrt{F^2(x) + H^2(x)}}{\sum_n A_n(x) + \varepsilon}, \tag{9}$$

where ε is a small positive constant.

In order to calculate the quadrature pair of filters M_n^e and M_n^o, Gabor filters (Gabor, 1946) or log-Gabor filters (Mancas-Thillou & Gosselin, 2006) can be applied. In this chapter, we use log-Gabor filters (e.g., wavelets at scale $n = 4$) due to its following two features: (i) log-Gabor filters, by definition, have no direct current (DC) component; and (ii) the transfer function of the log-Gabor filter has an extended tail at the high frequency end, which makes it more capable to encode natural images than ordinary Gabor filters (Zhang *et al.*, 2011). The transfer function of a log-Gabor filter in the frequency domain is

$$G(\omega) = e^{-\frac{[\log(\omega/\omega_0)]^2}{2\sigma_r^2}}, \tag{10}$$

where ω_0 is the filter's center frequency and σ_r controls the filter's bandwidth.

To compute the PCM of two-dimensional (2D) grayscale images, we can apply the 1D analysis over several orientations and then combine the results according to some rules. The 1D log-Gabor filters described above can be extended to 2D ones by applying Gaussian function across the filter perpendicular to its orientation (Kovesi, 1999; Fischer *et al.*, 2007; Wang *et al.*, 2008). The 2D log-Gabor function has the following transfer function

$$G_2(\omega,\theta_j) = e^{-\frac{[\log(\omega/\omega_0)]^2}{2\sigma_r^2}} \cdot e^{-\frac{(\theta-\theta_j)^2}{2\sigma_\theta^2}}, \tag{11}$$

where θ_j=$(j\pi)/(2J)$ and $j = 0, 1, 2,..., J$–1. J is the number of orientations and σ_θ determines the filter's angular bandwidth. By modulating ω_0 and θ_j and convolving G_2 with the 2D image, we get a set of responses at each point (x, y) as $e_{n,\theta_j}(x,y), o_{n,\theta_j}(x,y)]$. The local amplitude at scale n and orientation θ_j is

$$A_{n,\theta_j} = \sqrt{e_{n,\theta_j}^2(x,y) + o_{n,\theta_j}^2(x,y)}. \tag{12}$$

and the local energy along orientation θ_j is

$$E_{\theta_j} = \sqrt{F_{\theta_j}^2(x,y) + H_{\theta_j}^2(x,y)}. \tag{13}$$

where

$$F_{\theta_j}(x,y) = \sum_n e_{n,\theta_j}(x,y), \ H_{\theta_j}(x,y) = \sum_n o_{n,\theta_j}(x,y). \tag{14}$$

The two-dimensional *PCM* at (x, y) is defined as

$$PC_{2D}(x,y)=\frac{\sum_{j}E_{\theta_j}(x,y)}{\sum_{n}\sum_{j}A_{n,\theta_j}(x,y)+\varepsilon}, \tag{15}$$

where ε is a small positive constant. It should be noted that $PC_{2D}(x,y)$ is a real number within [0,1]. The phase congruency metric (PCM) of an image is defined as

$$PCM=\frac{1}{MN}\sum_{(x,y)}PC_{2D}(x,y)=\frac{1}{MN}\sum_{(x,y)}\frac{\sum_{j}E_{\theta_j}(x,y)}{\sum_{n}\sum_{j}A_{n,\theta_j}(x,y)+\varepsilon}, \tag{16}$$

where $M{\times}N$ is the size of the image. The range of PCM is [0,1].

3.2. Gradient Magnitude Metric (GMM)

The image *gradient magnitude* (GM) is computed to encode contrast information. PC and GM are complementary and they reflect different aspects of the HVS (human visual system) in assessing the local image quality. The GM measures the sharpness of an image. The perception of sharpness is related to the clarity of detail of an image. Image gradient computation is a traditional topic in image processing. Gradient operators can be expressed by convolution masks. One of commonly used gradient operators is the Sobel operator. The partial derivatives of image $f(x, y)$, G_x and G_y, along horizontal and vertical directions using the Sobel operators are

$$G_x=\frac{1}{4}\begin{bmatrix}1 & 0 & -1\\ 2 & 0 & -2\\ 1 & 0 & -1\end{bmatrix}*f(x,y),\ \ G_y=\frac{1}{4}\begin{bmatrix}1 & 2 & 1\\ 0 & 0 & 0\\ -1 & -2 & -1\end{bmatrix}*f(x,y) \tag{17}$$

The GM of $f(x, y)$ at pixel (x, y) is defined as

$$G(x,y)=\sqrt{G_x^2+G_y^2}. \tag{18}$$

The averaged GM over all pixels is called image *gradient magnitude metric* (GMM),

$$GMM=\frac{1}{MN}\sum_{x,y}G(x,y)=\frac{1}{MN}\sum_{x,y}\sqrt{G_x^2+G_y^2}, \tag{19}$$

where $M \times N$ is the size of the image.

3.3. Image Contrast Metric (ICM)

An image with excellent contrast has a wide dynamic range of intensity level and appropriate intensity. Both the dynamic range of intensity level or the overall intensity distribution of the image can be provided by a histogram. A global contrast metric is proposed using the histogram character. The histogram of image with levels in the range [0, N-1] is a frequency-distribution function defined as the overall intensity distribution of an image

$$h(X_k) = n_k, \tag{20}$$

where X_k is the k-th level of input and n_k is the number of the pixels in the image having level x_k. The probability density function (PDF) is computed by

$$P(X_k) = n_k / n, \tag{21}$$

where n is the total number of the pixels of the image. The dynamic range value β is defined as

$$\beta = \sum_{k=0}^{L-1} S(X_k), \tag{22}$$

where

$$S(X_k) = \begin{cases} 1, & if\ P(X_k) > 0 \\ 0, & otherwise \end{cases}. \tag{23}$$

The dynamic range matrix α of histogram is defined as

$$\alpha = \frac{\beta}{2N - \beta}, \tag{24}$$

where $\alpha \in [0,1]$ and a larger value of α means a wider dynamic range in the histogram, which leads to better contrast. The image contrast metric is defined as

$$C = \alpha \sum_{k=0}^{N-1} \frac{X_k}{N} P(X_k). \tag{25}$$

For color images, the image contrast metric is determined by both gray contrast and color contrast. Because human perception is more sensitive to the luminance on contrast evaluation, we employ L^* channel in the CIELAB space to evaluate the color contrast. Thus, image contrast is determined by the histogram of gray intensity and the histogram of color luminance L^* (see Fig. 1). For the gray intensity I, the gray contrast metric is defined as

$$C_g = \alpha_I \sum_{k=0}^{N_I - 1} \frac{I_k}{N} P(I_k), \tag{26}$$

where α_I and $P(I_k)$ can be calculated as above for gray intensity. For L^* channel, the color contrast metric is

$$C_c = \alpha_c \sum_{k=0}^{N_{L^*} - 1} \frac{L_k^*}{N_{L^*}} P(L_k^*), \tag{27}$$

where α_c and $P(L_k)$ can be calculated as above for L^* channel. The global *image contrast metric* (ICM) is defined as

$$ICM = \sqrt{\omega_1 C_g^2 + \omega_2 C_c^2}, \tag{28}$$

where ω_1 and ω_2 are the weights of C_g and C_c. For simplicity, we choose $\omega_1 = \omega_2 = 0.5$. *ICM* varies within [0,1]. The evaluation of image contrast metric of color fusion image is shown in Fig. 1.

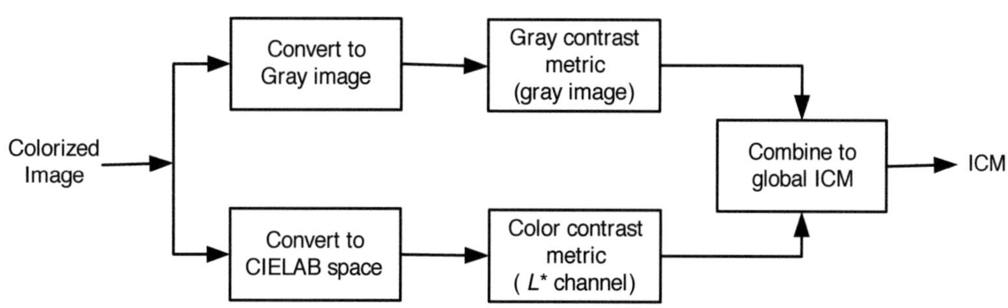

Figure 1. Diagram of calculation of the contrast metric.

3.4. Color Natural Metric (CNM)

Given a daylight image $f_1(x, y)$ and a colorized image $f_2(x, y)$, if a colorized image is similar to the daylight image then the colorized image is considered as of a good quality. Since a human is sensitive to hue in addition to luminance, we compare the a^* and b^* channels of the reference image with that of the colorized image using the gray relational analysis (GRA) theory (Ma *et al.*, 2005).

We first convert two images, f_1 and f_2, to $L^*a^*b^*$ space. $L_i(x,y)$, $a_i(x,y)$, and $b_i(x,y)$ are the $L^*a^*b^*$ values of f_i at pixel (x, y). The gray relation coefficient between a_1 and a_2 at pixel (x, y) is defined as

$$\xi_a(x,y)=\frac{\min_i\min_j|a_1^*(i,j)-a_2^*(i,j)|+0.5\max_i\max_j|a_1^*(i,j)-a_2^*(i,j)|}{|a_1^*(x,y)-a_2^*(x,y)|+0.5\max_i\max_j|a_1^*(i,j)-a_2^*(i,j)|+\varepsilon}, \tag{29}$$

where ε is a small positive constant.

The gray relation coefficient between b_1 and b_2 at pixel (x, y) is defined as

$$\xi_b(x,y)=\frac{\min_i\min_j|b_1^*(i,j)-b_2^*(i,j)|+0.5\max_i\max_j|b_1^*(i,j)-b_2^*(i,j)|}{|b_1^*(x,y)-b_2^*(x,y)|+0.5\max_i\max_j|b_1^*(i,j)-b_2^*(i,j)|+\varepsilon}. \tag{30}$$

In the definitions of $\xi_a(x,y)$ and $\xi_b(x,y)$, min() and max() are operated over whole image. However, it is possible that min() and max() are operated over a small neighborhood of (x, y).

The gray rational degrees of a^* and b^* information for two images are defined as

$$R_a=\sum_{(x,y)}\omega(x,y)\xi_a(x,y), \tag{31}$$

$$R_b=\sum_{(x,y)}\omega(x,y)\xi_b(x,y), \tag{32}$$

where $\omega(x,y)$ is the weight of the gray rational coefficient, which satisfies

$$\sum_{(x,y)}\omega(x,y)=1. \tag{33}$$

For simplicity, we choose $\omega(x,y)=\frac{1}{M\times N}$ where M and N are the length of vectors x and y respectively.

The *color natural metric* (CNM) is defined as

$$CNM=\sqrt{R_aR_b}. \tag{34}$$

CNM varies within [0,1]; the larger the CNM, the more similar the two images.

4. Objective Evaluation Index (OEI)

With the four metrics defined in Section 3, a new *objective evaluation index* (OEI) is proposed to quantitatively evaluate the qualities of colorized images. Given the reference image f_1 and the colorized image f_2, the OEI is calcualted in two steps. First the local similarity maps of the two images are computed, and then the similarity maps are integrated into a single similarity score.

The two images are first converted into $L^*a^*b^*$ space. For L^* information, the PC maps are calculated and denoted as PC_1 and PC_2 for f_1 and f_2 images, respectively. The similarity measure between PC_1 and PC_2 at pixel (x, y) is defined as

$$S_{PC}(x,y)=\frac{2PC_1(x,y)PC_2(x,y)+K_1}{PC_1^2(x,y)+PC_2^2(x,y)+K_1}, \tag{35}$$

where K_1 is a positive constant. In practice, the determination of K_1 depends on the dynamic range of PC values. S_{PC} varies within [0,1]. Similarly, the similarity measure based on the two GM values is defined as

$$S_G(x,y)=\frac{2G_1(x,y)G_2(x,y)+K_2}{G_1^2(x,y)+G_2^2(x,y)+K_2}, \tag{36}$$

where K_2 is a positive constant. S_G varies within [0,1]. Then, $S_{PC}(x,y)$ and $S_G(x,y)$ are combined into one similarity measure, $S_L\ (x)$, as follows

$$S_L(x,y)=[S_{PC}(x,y)]^{\lambda_1}[S_G(x,y)]^{\lambda_2}, \tag{37}$$

where λ_1 and λ_2 are parameters to adjust the relative importance of PC and GM features.

With the aid of the similarity $S_L\ (x,y)$ at each pixel (x, y), the overall similarity between f_1 and f_2 can be calculated with the averaged $S_L\ (x,y)$ over all pixels. However, the image saliency (i.e., local significance) usually varies with the pixel location. For example, edges convey more crucial information than smooth areas. Specifically, a human is sensitive to phase congruent structures (Henriksson *et al.*, 2009), and thus a larger $PC(x, y)$ value between f_1 and f_2 implies a higher impact on evaluating the similarity between f_1 and f_2 at location (x, y). Therefore, we use $PC_{\max}(x,y)=max[PC_1(x,y), PC_2(x,y)]$ to weigh the importance of $S_L\ (x,y)$ in formulating the overall similarity. Accordingly, the objective evaluation index (OEI) between f_1 and f_2 is defined as follows

$$OEI=\left(\frac{\sum_{(x,y)} PC_{\max}(x,y)S_L(x,y)}{\sum_{(x,y)} PC_{\max}(x,y)}\right)^{\gamma_1}\times(S_{ICM})^{\gamma_2}\times(CNM)^{\gamma_3}, \tag{38}$$

where

$$PC_{\max}(x,y) = \max[PC_1(x,y), PC_2(x,y)], \tag{39}$$

$$S_{ICM} = \frac{2ICM(f_1) \times ICM(f_2) + K_3}{ICM(f_1)^2 + ICM(f_2)^2 + K_3}, \tag{40}$$

where CNM is previously defined and K_3 and γ_i ($i = 1,2,3$) are positive constants. The diagram of calculating OEI is shown in Fig. 2. The range of OEI is [0,1]. The larger the OEI value of a colorized image is, the more similar (i.e., the better) the colorized image is to the reference image. *Error pooling* is the integration of methods with tradeoffs between γ_1, γ_2, and γ_3.

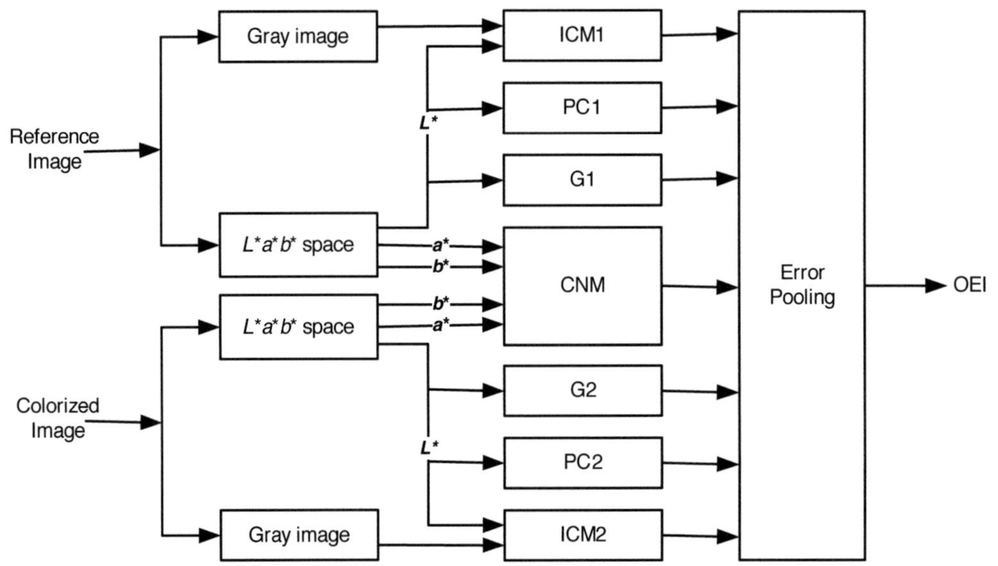

Figure 2. Diagram of calculating OEI in $L^*a^*b^*$ space.

γ_1, γ_2, and γ_3 are the weights of three components in the OEI metric. Selection of γ_i is critical for the OEI calculation. The values of γ_i are empirically decided, and the typical values of γ_1 and γ_2 are between 0.8~1.1 and γ_3 is between 0.05~0.2. K_i ($i = 1,2,3$) are constants to increase the metric stability. In our experiments presented in Section 6, we chose γ_1=γ_2= 1, γ_3= 0.2; $K_1 = 0.85$, $K_2 = 160$, $K_3 = 0.001$; and $\lambda_1 = \lambda_2 = 1$.

5. Experimental results and discussions

In our experiments, five triplets of multispectral NV images (as shown in Figs. 3-7; collected at Alcorn State University), color RGB, near infrared (NIR) and long wave infrared (LWIR), were colorized by using six different coloring methods as described in Section 2. The three-band input images are shown in Figs. 3-7a, b and c, respectively. The image resolutions and its taken time are given in figure captions. The RGB images and LWIR images were taken by a FLIR SC620 two-in-one camera, which has LWIR camera (of 640×480 pixel original resolution and 7.5~13 μm spectral range) and an integrated visible-band digital camera (2048×1536 pixel original resolution). The NIR images were taken by a FLIR SC6000 camera (640×512 pixel original resolution and 0.9~1.7 μm spectral range). Two cameras (SC620 and SC6000) were placed on the same fixture and turned to aim at the same location. The images were typically captured during sunset time and dusk time during a fall season. One exception is shown in Fig. 7, which was taken at noon time.

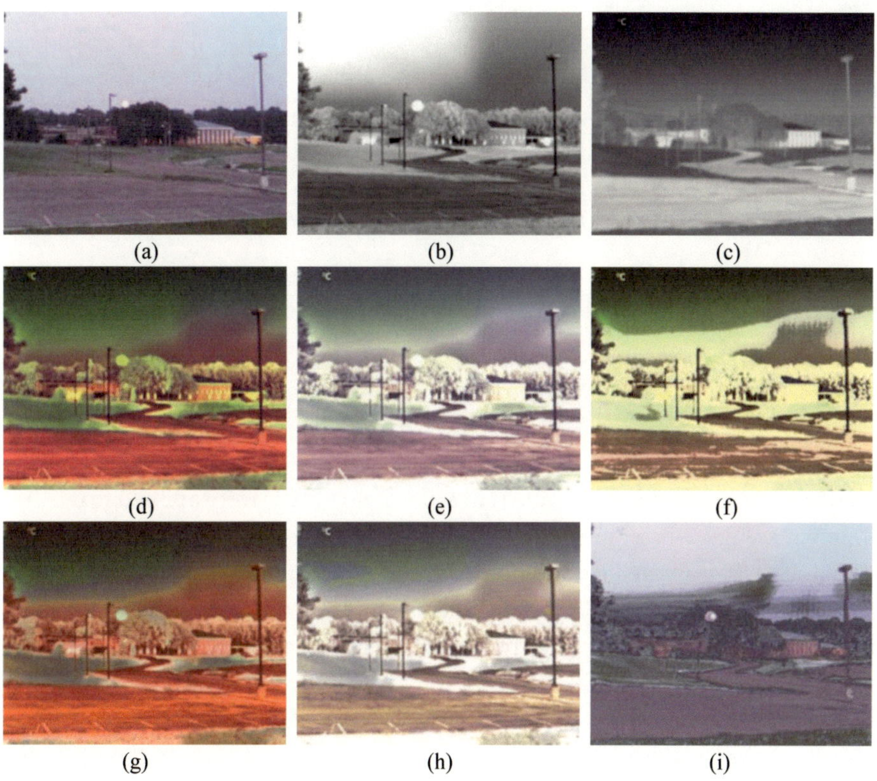

Figure 3. Night-vision coloring comparison (Case# AT008 – taken at sunset time; 640×480 pixels): (a-c) Color RGB, NIR, and LWIR images, respectively; (d-f) The colorized images using channel-based color fusion of (NIR⊕ LWIR), statistic-matching, and histogram-matching, respectively; (g-i) The colorized images using joint-HM, stat-match then joint-HM, and LUT-mapping, respectively. The settings in the color-mappings of (e-i) are source = (d) and target = (a). Notice that the contrasts of all color images were increased by 10%, and the brightness of (a) and (i) were increased by 10%.

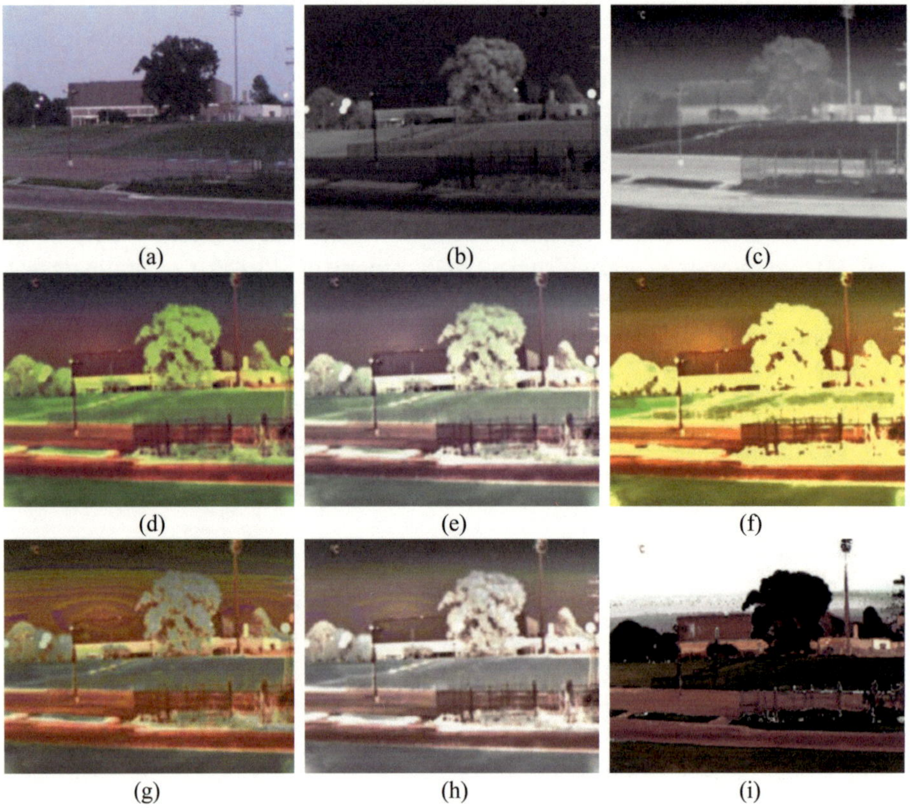

Figure 4. Night-vision coloring comparison (Case# AT009 – taken after sunset time; 640×480 pixels): (a-c) Color RGB, NIR, and LWIR images, respectively; (d-f) The colorized images using channel-based color fusion of (NIR⊕ LWIR), statistic-matching, and histogram-matching, respectively; (g-i) The colorized images using joint-HM, stat-match then joint-HM, and LUT-mapping, respectively. The settings in the color-mappings of (e-i) are source = (d) and target = (a). Notice that the contrasts of all color images were increased by 10%, and the brightness of (a) was increased by 10%.

Of course, image registration and fusion (Hil & Batchelor, 2001) were applied to the three band images shown in Figs. 3-7, where manual alignment was employed to the RGB image shown in Figs. 5-6a since they are so dark and noisy. To better present the color images (including the daylight RGB images and the colorized NV images), contrast and brightness adjustments (as described in figure captions) were applied. Notice that piecewise contrast stretching (Eq. (2)) was used for NIR enhancement. As referred in Eq. (1d), the fused images (shown elsewhere (Zheng & Essock, 2008)) were obtained using the *a*DWT algorithm (Zheng *et al.*, 2005). The channel-based color fusion (CBCF, defined in Eqs. (1)) was applied to the NIR and LWIR images (shown in Figs. 3-7b & c), and the results are illustrated in Figs. 3-7d. The resulted images from two-band color fusion (Figs. 3-7d) resemble natural colors, which makes scene classification easier. The paved ground appears reddish since they have strong heat radiations (at dusk time) and thus causes strong responses in LWIR images. In the color-fusion images, the trees, buildings and grasses can be easily distinguished from ground (parking lots) and

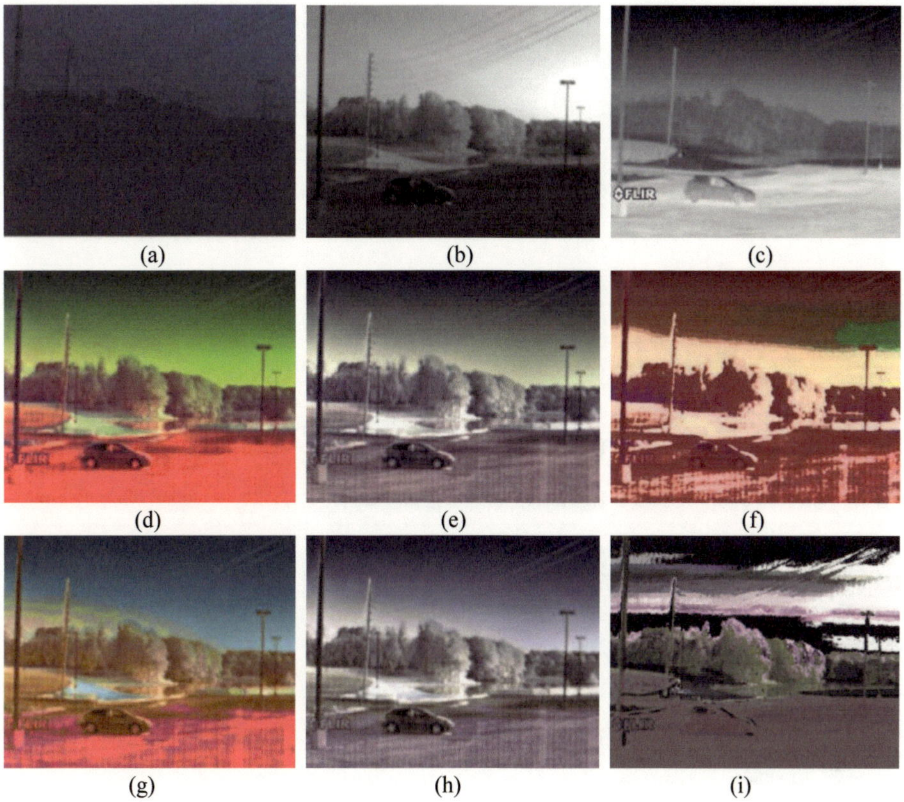

Figure 5. Night-vision coloring comparison (Case# AT012 – taken at dusk time; 640×480 pixels): (a-c) Color RGB, NIR, and LWIR images, respectively; (d-f) The colorized images using channel-based color fusion of (NIR⊕ LWIR), statistic-matching, and histogram-matching, respectively; (g-i) The colorized images using joint-HM, stat-match then joint-HM, and LUT-mapping, respectively. The settings in the color-mappings of (e-i) are source = (d) and target = Fig. 8(a) due to the dark RGB image in (a). Notice that the contrasts of all color images were increased by 10%, and the brightness of (a) and (i) were increased by 20% and 10%, respectively.

sky. For example, the car is clearly identified in Fig. 5d, where the water area (between ground and trees and shown in cyan color) is certainly noticeable. However, it is hard to realize any water area in the original images (Figs. 5a-c).

All color mapping methods were applied to the five triplets and their results are presented in Figs. 3-7. The source images are the color-fusion images (Figs. 3-7d), while the target images are the color RGB images (Figs. 3-4a & Fig. 8a-b). Figs. 5-6a cannot be used as the target images since they are too dark and noisy. Figs. 3-7e show the colored images with the statistic matching (SM) method, which are more similar to the daylight pictures in contrast with the color-fusion images. The five results (Figs. 3-7e) are equivalently good, which means that the statistic matching is reliable. The histogram matching (HM) results shown in Figs. 3-7f are oversaturated, which may be more suitable for segmentation-based colorization (Zheng & Essock, 2008). The joint histogram matching (JHM) are illustrated in Figs. 3-7g, where the mapped

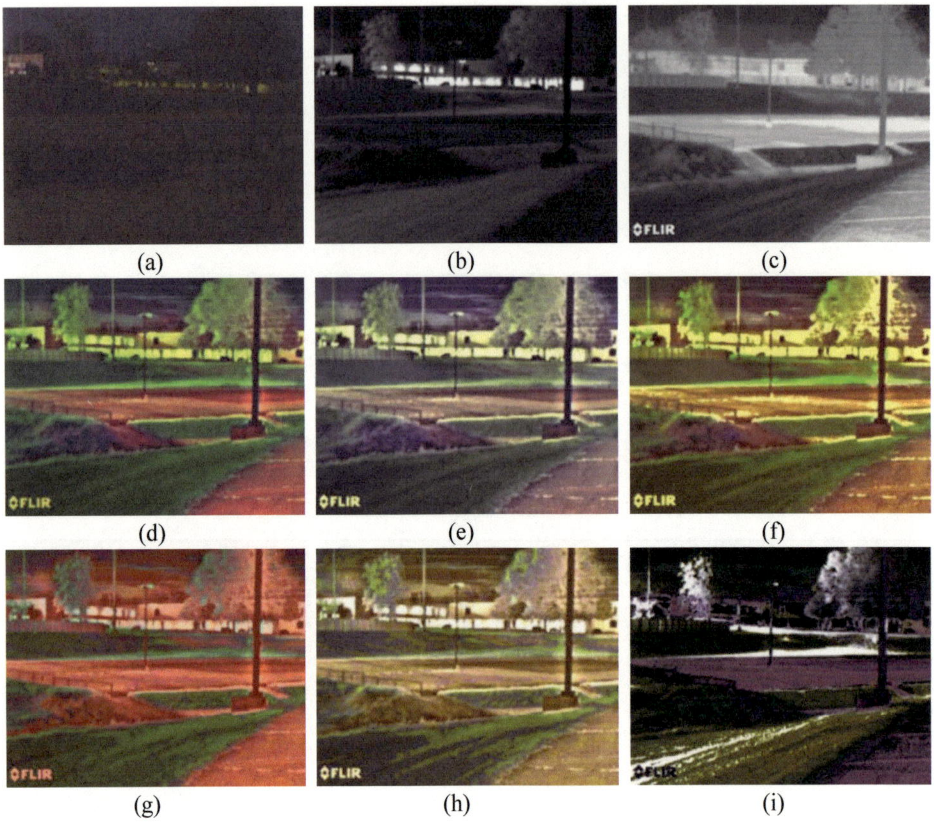

Figure 6. Night-vision coloring comparison (Case# ST029 – taken at dusk time; 640×480 pixels): (a-c) Color RGB, NIR, and LWIR images, respectively; (d-f) The colorized images using channel-based color fusion of (NIR⊕ LWIR), statistic-matching, and histogram-matching, respectively; (g-i) The colorized images using joint-HM, stat-match then joint-HM, and LUT-mapping, respectively. The settings in the color-mappings of (e-i) are source = (d) and target = Fig. 8(b) due to the dark RGB image in (a). Notice that the contrasts of (d-i) were increased by 10%, and (a) was increased by 20%. The brightness of (a) and (i) were increased by 20% and 10%, respectively.

images are better than the color fusions but preserve much reddish colors (existed in source images). The "stat-match then joint-HM" (SM-JHM) means that a joint-HM is performed with inputs of (source = the SM-colored image in Fig. 3e; target = the RGB image in Fig. 3a). The SM-JHM results are presented in Figs. 3-7h, which sometimes are better than the results from either stat-match or joint-HM (e.g., Fig. 3h). The examples of LUT-mapping colorization are given in Figs. 3-7i. Figs. 3-4i and Fig. 7i (an ideal case of LUT mapping) shows impressive colors; whereas Figs. 5-6i exhibit noisy and distorted since the reference images (shown in Figs. 8a-b) are misaligned with the NV images (shown in Figs. 5-6). When using the LUT established in a different case at daytime (aiming at different direction at nighttime), the more misalignment the worse the LUT-colored results appear. The LUT-based colorization described in Subsection 2.6 is perhaps suitable for a surveillance application where a camera is aiming at a fixed direction.

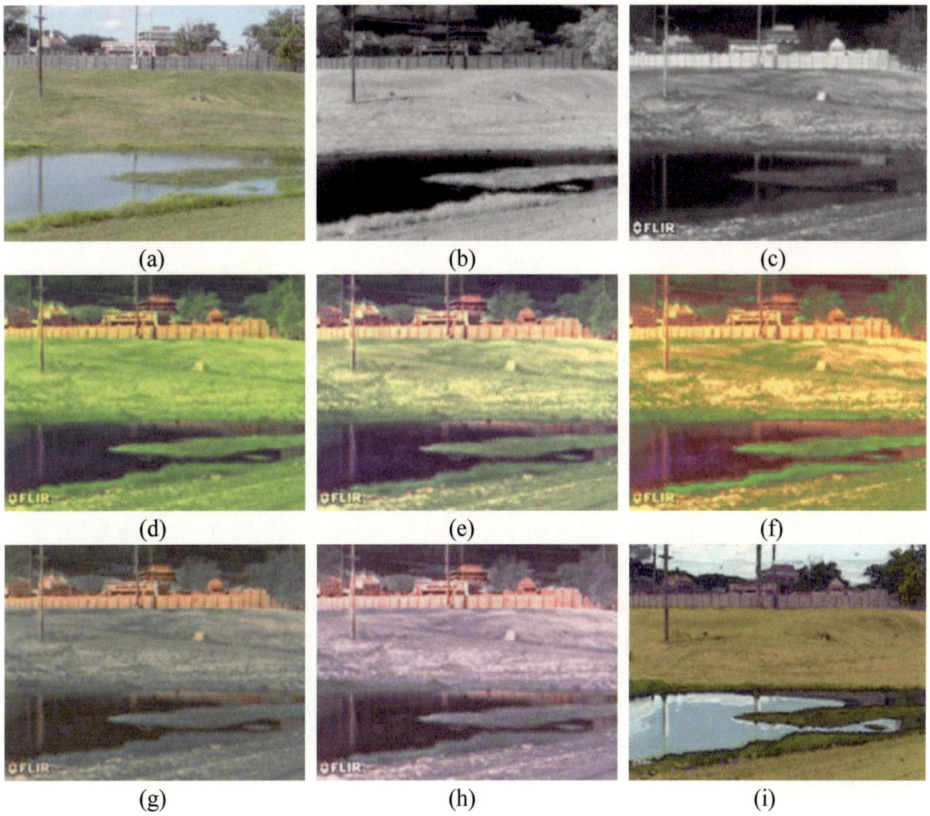

Figure 7. Night-vision coloring comparison (Case# ST102 – taken at noon time; 640×480 pixels): (a-c) Color RGB, NIR, and LWIR images, respectively; (d-f) The colorized images using channel-based color fusion of (NIR⊕ LWIR), statistic-matching, and histogram-matching, respectively; (g-i) The colorized images using joint-HM, stat-match then joint-HM, and LUT-mapping, respectively. The settings in the color-mappings of (e-i) are source = (d) and target = (a).

Figure 8. Color RGB images for night-vision colorization (taken before sunset time; 640×480 pixels): (a) from Case# AT002 (target of Fig. 5, AT012); (b) from Case# ST014 (target of Fig. 6, ST029). Notice that their contrasts were increased by 10%.

Visual inspections of colorized images can generally tell which one is better or the best when there are big enough differences between several versions of colorized images. For example, casual inspections may easily confirm that, top 3 methods are SM, SM-JHM, and LUT; HM and JHM are poor; and CBCF is medium. However, the subjective evalutions become more and more difficult with a larger number of color images and also hard with small or diverse differences. In other words, it is hard for subjective evalutions to give an exact order of six colroziation methods. Let us examine the objective evaluations.

The objective evaluations using the OEI metric defined in Eq. (14) (refer to Section 4) are presented in Table 1 (corresponding to Figs. 3-7 respectively), where the orders of metric values (1 for the smallest OEI) are given within round parentheses. Keep in mind that, the larger the OEI value of a colorized image is, the better quality (i.e., the higher order number) the colorized image has. According to the OEI values in Table 1, the quality order of colorized images varies with figures (cases). To have an overall impression, the sums of the order numbers in five cases (i.e., Figs. 3-7) are calculated and shown at the rightmost column in Table 1. The quality order of each colorization method (6 for the best) is given within the curly brackets. The order of colorization methods from the best to the worst: SM (stat-match), SM-JHM (stat-match then joint-HM), LUT, CBCF (channel-based color fusion), HM (histogram matching), JHM (joint-HM). This order sorted by OEI values is quite consistent with the order of subjective evaluations.

Method (Plot)	Fig. 3 (AT008)	Fig. 4 (AT009)	Fig. 5 (AT012)	Fig. 6 (ST029)	Fig. 7 (ST102)	Sum {Order}
CBCF (d)	0.4753 (3)	0.5497 (3)	0.5178 (2)	0.5132 (4)	0.5872 (3)	15 {3}
SM (e)	0.5470 (6)	0.6022 (5)	0.6058 (6)	0.5529 (5)	0.6337 (6)	**28 {6}**
HM (f)	0.4519 (2)	0.4890 (1)	0.3587 (1)	0.5099 (3)	0.5736 (2)	9 {2}
JHM (g)	0.4372 (1)	0.5250 (2)	0.5189 (3)	0.4674 (1)	0.5503 (1)	8 {1}
SM-JHM (h)	0.5428 (5)	0.5954 (4)	0.5978 (5)	0.5678 (6)	0.6154 (4)	*24 {5}*
LUT (i)	0.5148 (4)	0.6025 (6)	0.5238 (4)	0.4882 (2)	0.6322 (5)	21 {4}

Table 1. The OEI (Order) values of six color-mapping methods over five cases shown in Figs. 3-7 (The Sum & {Order} at last colmun is calculated with the orders of five cases).

The subjective evaluations of night vision coloration are based on casual visual inspections. More qualitative measurements, subjective evaluations (by a group of subjects), and statistical analysis will be introduced in the future. The quantitative (objective) evaluations using the objective quality index (OEI) require a reference (daylight) image. Thus we will continuously improve the OEI metric by relaxing the requirement of a reference image. We will further conduct more comprehensive comparisons.

http://dx.doi.org/10.5772/56948

6. Conclusions

In this chapter, we review six night-vision colorization techniques, a channel-based color fusion (CBCF) procedure; statistic matching (SM), histogram matching (HM), joint histogram matching (JHM), and stat-match then joint-HM (SM-JHM) method, and LUT-based approaches. An objective evaluation metric for NV colorization, objective evaluation index (OEI), is introduced. The experimental results with five case analyses showed the order of colorization methods from the best to the worst: SM, SM-JHM, LUT, CBCF, HM, JHM. The order of objective evaluations comply with the order of subjective evaluations.

The accurate objective metric such as OEI will help develop, select, and/or tune up a better NV colorization technique. The ideally colorized NV imagery can significantly enhance the night vision targeting by human users and will eventually lead to improved performance of remote sensing, nighttime perception, and situational awareness.

Acknowledgements

This research is supported by the U. S. Army Research Office under grant number W911NF-08-1-0404.

Author details

Yufeng Zheng[1*], Wenjie Dong[2], Genshe Chen[3] and Erik P. Blasch[4]

*Address all correspondence to: Yufeng.Zheng@R2Image.com

1 Alcorn State University, USA

2 The University of Texas-Pan American, USA

3 I-Fusion Technologies, Inc, USA

4 US Air Force Research Laboratory, USA

References

[1] Alparone, L.; Baronti, S.; Garzelli, A.; & Nencini, F. (2004). A global quality measurement of Pan-sharpened multispectral imagery, *IEEE Geosci. Remote Sens. Lett.*, 1(4), 313-317.

[2] Blasch, E.; Li X.; Chen, G. & Li, W. (2008). Image Quality Assessment for Performance Evaluation of Image Fusion, *Proc. of 11th international conference on Information fusion*, Germany.

[3] Essock, E. A.; Sinai, M. J. & et al. (1999). Perceptual ability with real-world nighttime scenes: imageintensified, infrared, and fused-color imagery, *Hum. Factors* 41(3), 438–452.

[4] Fischer, S.; Sroubek, F.; Perrinet, L.; Redondo, R. & Cristoal, G. (2007). Self-invertible 2D log-Gabor wavelets, *Int. J. Computer Vision*, 75(2), 231-246.

[5] Gabor, D. (1946). Theory of communication, *J. Inst. Elec. Eng.*, 93(3), 429-457.

[6] Gonzalez, R. C. & Woods, R. E. (2002). *Digital Image Processing* (Second Edition), Prentice Hall, ISBN: 0201180758, Upper Saddle River, NJ.

[7] Henriksson, L.; Hyvarinen, A. & Vanni, S. (2009). Representation of cross-frequency spatial phase relationships in human visual cortex, *J. Neuroscience*, 29(45), 14342-14351.

[8] Hill, D. L. G. & Batchelor P. (2001). Registration methodology: concepts and algorithms, in Medical Image Registration, Hajnal, J. V.; Hill, D. L. G.; & Hawkes, D. J. Eds, Boca Raton, FL.

[9] Hogervorst, M.A. & Toet, A. (2008). Method for applying daytime colors to nighttime imagery in realtime, *Proc. SPIE 6974*, 697403.

[10] Kovesi, P. (1999) . Image features from phase congruency, Videre: *J. Comp. Vis. Res.*, 1(3), 1-26.

[11] Liu, Z.; Blasch, E.; Xue, Z.; Langaniere, R.; & Wu, R (2012). Objective Assessment of Multiresolution Image Fusion Algorithms for Context Enhancement in Night Vision: A Comparative Survey, *IEEE Trans. Pattern Analysis and Machine Intelligence*, 34(1): 94-109.

[12] Ma, M.; Tian, H.P.; & Hao, C.Y. (2005). New method to quality evaluation for image fusion using gray relational analysis, *Opt. Eng.* 44, 087010.

[13] Malacara, D. (2002) Color Vision and Colorimetry: Theory and Applications, SPIE Press, Bellingham, WA.

[14] Mancas-Thillou, C. & Gosselin, B. (2006). Character segmentation-by-recognition using log-Gabor filters, *Proc. Int. Conf. Pattern Recognition*, 901-904.

[15] Morrone, M.C.; Ross, J.; Burr, D.C.; & Owens, R. (1986) Mach bands are phase dependent, *Nature*, 324 (6049), 250-253.

[16] Toet, A. (2003). Natural colour mapping for multiband nightvision imagery, *Information Fusion* 4, 155-166.

[17] Toet, A. & Hogervorst , M.A. (2012). Progress in color night vision," *Opt. Eng.* 51 (1), 010901.

[18] Toet, A. & IJspeert, J. K. (2001). Perceptual evaluation of different image fusion schemes, in: I. Kadar (Ed.), *Signal Processing, Sensor Fusion, and Target Recognition X*, The International Society for Optical Engineering, Bellingham, WA, pp.436–441.

[19] Tsagaris, V. (2009). Objective evaluation of color image fusion methods, *Opt. Eng.* 48, 066201.

[20] Tsagaris, V. & Anastassopoulos, V. (2006) "Global measure for assessing image fusion methods," *Opt. Eng.* 45, 026201.

[21] Varga, J. T. (1999). Evaluation of operator performance using true color and artificial color in natural scene perception (Report ADA363036), Naval Postgraduate School, Monterey, CA.

[22] Wald, L. ; Ranchin, T. ; & Mangolini, M. (1997). Fusion of satellite images of different spatial resolutions: assessing the quality of resulting images, *Photogramm. Eng. Remote Sens.* 63(6), 691-699.

[23] Wang, W.; Li, J.; Huang, F.; & Feng, H. (2008). Design and implementation of log-Gabor filter in fingerprint image enhancement, *Pattern Recognit. Letters*, 29(3), 301-308.

[24] Waxman, A.M.; Gove, A. N. & *et al.* (1996). Progress on color night vision: visible/IR fusion, perception and search, and low-light CCD imaging, *Proc. SPIE Vol. 2736*, pp. 96-107, Enhanced and Synthetic Vision 1996, Jacques G. Verly; Ed.

[25] Yuan, Y.; Zhang, J.; Chang, B.; & Han Y. (2011). Objective quality evaluation of visible and infrared color fusion image, *Opt. Eng.*, 50(3), 033202.

[26] Zhang, L.; Zhang, L.; Mou, X. & Zhang, D. (2011) FSIM: A Feature Similarity Index for Image Quality Assessment, *IEEE Trans. on Image Processing*, 20 (8), 2378 - 2386.

[27] Zheng, Y. (2011). A channel-based color fusion technique using multispectral images for night vision enhancement, *Proc. SPIE 8135*, 813511.

[28] Zheng, Y. (2012). An Overview of Night Vision Colorization Techniques using Multispectral Images: from Color Fusion to Color Mapping", 2012 International Conference on Audio, Language and Image Processing (ICALIP 2012), Shanghai, China.

[29] Zheng, Y. & Essock, E. A. (2008). A local-coloring method for night-vision colorization utilizing image analysis and image fusion, *Information Fusion* 9, 186-199.

[30] Zheng, Y.; Essock, E. A. & Hansen, B. C. (2005). An advanced DWT fusion algorithm and its optimization by using the metric of image quality index, *Optical Engineering* 44 (3), 037003-1-12.

[31] Zheng, Y; Dong, W.; & Blasch, E. (2012). Qualitative and quantitative comparisons of multispectral night vision colorization techniques," Optical Engineering, 51(8), 087004

[32] Zheng, Y; Reese, K; Blasch, E; & McManamon, P. (2013). Qualitative evaluations and comparisons of six night-vision colorization methods, Proc. SPIE 8745.

Chapter 6

A Trous Wavelet and Image Fusion

Shaohui Chen

Additional information is available at the end of the chapter

http://dx.doi.org/10.5772/56947

1. Introduction

1.1. Introduction to the à trous wavelet

In 1992, Mallat and Zhong designed a fast algorithm for the orthogonal wavelet transform (OWT) of a discrete signal $f_0(x)$ having finite energy by level filtering with a brace of low-filter $h(n)$ and high-pass filter $g(n)$. For the original image A_0, the OWT can be achieved as:

$$\begin{cases} A_r(i,j) = \sum_{m,n\in z} h(m)h(n)A_{r-1}(2i-m,2j-n) \\ D_r^1(i,j) = \sum_{m,n\in z} h(m)\tilde{g}(n)A_{r-1}(2i-m,2j-n) \\ D_r^2(i,j) = \sum_{m,n\in z} \tilde{g}(m)h(n)A_{r-1}(2i-m,2j-n) \\ D_r^3(i,j) = \sum_{m,n\in z} \tilde{g}(m)\tilde{g}(n)A_{r-1}(2i-m,2j-n) \end{cases} \tag{1}$$

The reconstruction can be achieved by the inverse OWT (IOWT) as:

$$\begin{aligned} A_{r-1}(i,j) = 4\sum_{m,n\in z} h(m)h(n)A_r\left[\frac{i-m}{2},\frac{j-n}{2}\right] + \\ 4\sum_{m,n\in z} h(m)g(n)D_r^1\left[\frac{i-m}{2},\frac{j-n}{2}\right] + \\ 4\sum_{m,n\in z} g(m)h(n)D_r^2\left[\frac{i-m}{2},\frac{j-n}{2}\right] + \\ 4\sum_{m,n\in z} g(m)g(n)D_r^3\left[\frac{i-m}{2},\frac{j-n}{2}\right] \end{aligned} \tag{2}$$

In (1) and (2), r=1, 2,..., N denotes the decomposition levels, $\tilde{h}(m)$ and $\tilde{g}(m)$ are the conjugate filters of $h(n)$ and $g(n)$. A_r denotes the low frequency component of A_0 in horizontal and vertical direction. Similarly, D_r^1, D_r^2, D_r^3 respectively denote the horizontal low frequency and vertical high frequency component, the horizontal high frequency and vertical low frequency component, the horizontal high frequency and vertical high frequency component at resolution level r. High frequency component represent the detail and edge information while the low frequency component represent the coarse information.

As a simple example, the brace of low-filter $h(n)$ and high-pass filter $g(n)$ is given by $h(n)$=[0.7071, 0.7071], $g(n)$=[-0.7071, 0.7071].

The OWT is a popular method used for fusing multisensor images. The OWT decomposes an image with a wavelet basis according to pyramid scheme. The resolution is reduced by one-half at each level by subsampling data by two. One low frequency component, horizontal, vertical and diagonal detail components are produced at each level. The complete decomposition produces the same number of pixels as the original image.

The OWT can be used to improve the quality of the fused image. However, some limitations exist: 1) the OWT is applied to discrete images with sizes that are powers of two, because the resolution is reduced by two at each level. In this sense, it is not possible to fuse images of any sizes; 2) the analysis pixel by pixel is not possible since data are reduced at each resolution, it cannot follow to distinguish the evolution of a dominant feature through levels. 3) no satisfactory rule allowing a good quality of the fusion with the OWT exists (Chibani and Houacine, 2003).

For the OWT, the down-sampled multiresolution analysis does not preserve the translation invariance, *i.e.* a translation of the original signal does not necessarily imply a translation of the corresponding wavelet coefficients. Therefore, wavelet coefficients generated by an image discontinuity could disappear arbitrarily. This nonstationarity in the representation is a direct consequence of the downsampling operation. In order to preserve this property, stationary wavelet transform was introduced (Garzelli 2002). The redundant wavelet transform (RWT) overcomes the limits of the OWT, and allows a great flexibility in defining fusion rules. The RWT can be finished by using *à trous* (holes) algorithm as:

$$f_j(x) = \sum_n h(n) f_{j-1}(x + n2^{j-1}); j = 1, \cdots, J \tag{3}$$

$$\omega_j(x) = f_{j-1}(x) - f_j(x) = \sum_n g(n) f_{j-1}(x + n2^{j-1}); j = 1, \cdots J \tag{4}$$

The original signal can be reconstructed by adding the set of wavelet coefficients for all scales with the last approximation scale $f_J(x)$ as

$$f_0(x) = f_J(x) + \sum_{j=1}^{J} \omega_j(x) \tag{5}$$

The RWT of an image is accomplished by a separated fltering following rows and columns, respectively. Specifically, a single wavelet plane is produced at each scale by subtraction of two successive approximations without decimation. Hence, wavelet and approximation planes have the same dimensions as the original image.

A scaling function which has a B_3 cubic spline profile, and its use leads to a convolution with a mask of 5×5:

$$\frac{1}{256}\begin{pmatrix} 1 & 4 & 6 & 4 & 1 \\ 4 & 16 & 24 & 16 & 4 \\ 6 & 24 & 36 & 24 & 6 \\ 4 & 16 & 24 & 16 & 4 \\ 1 & 4 & 6 & 4 & 1 \end{pmatrix}$$

The RWT method is based on the fact that, in the RWT decomposition, the images are the successive versions of the original image at increasing scales. Thus, the first RWT planes of the high-resolution panchromatic image have spatial information that is not present in the multispectral image. The RWT based image fusion can be carried out using substitution method and additive method. In the wavelet substitution method, some of the RWT planes of the multispectral image are substituted by the RWT planes corresponding to the panchromatic image. In the additive method, the RWT planes of the panchromatic image are added to the multispectral image or to the intensity component of the multispectral images.

In the substitution method, the RWT planes of the multispectral image are discarded and substituted by the corresponding planes of the panchromatic image. While, in the additive method all the spatial information in the multispectral image is preserved, and the detail information from both sensors is used. The main difference between adding the panchromatic RWT planes to the multispectral images and to the intensity component is that in the first case, high frequency information is added to each multispectral image, while in the latter high frequency information modifies only the intensity. Thus, from the theoretical point of view, adding to the intensity component is a better choice than adding to each multispectral image (Núñez et al., 1999).

2. Multivalued wavelet transform

2.1. Feature space

Remote sensing image is the carrier of information by sampling the real valued function of space-time about the observed earth's surface. The digital number values of a remote sensing image have multivarious meanings, which include fractal geometry (Liu and Li 1997), raggedness of ground surface (Liu 2000), inner specialties (Eskicioglu and Fisher 1995), definition and contrast (Lu and Healy, Jr. 1994), and edge and boundary-dependent shape segmentation (Nikolov *et al.* 2000). They are displayed by the grey-values, the abstracted spectral reflectance, statistical elements, *e.g.*, mean and variance, the mutual relationship between neighborhood pixels, and grey-values of the same object, respectively. In the following text, these statistical attributes of the original image (I) are dissected into seven representative features with pseudo-formulae.

1. Setover: Setover (S) is an important connection between the specific observation of grey-value fluctuation and the usual intensity stability. It balances the total oscillation around the center by the absolute bias between each grey-value and the mean μ_I. Simultaneously it improves the confidence and sensitivity to locate abnormity by removing μ_I.

$$S = \left| I - \mu_I \right| \tag{6}$$

2. Visibility: Visibility (V) is defined inspired from the human visual system (Li *et al.* 2002) with μ_I and the standard deviation σ_I. Its each element is the contributive rate scaling local variety. It is equivalent to the deep projection of the corresponding setover onto σ_I.

$$V = \left(\frac{I - \mu_I}{\sigma_I} \right)^2 \tag{7}$$

3. Flat: The grey-values of a remote sensing image indirectly memorize the reflectance of the scanned groundcover by surveying device. In order to eliminate the possible influence of sunshine, namely the average intensity, flat (F) is defined according as each grey-value is divided by μ_I.

$$F = \frac{I}{\mu_I} \tag{8}$$

4. Gradient: Gradient (G) is pictured by the spatial frequency (Eskicioglu and Fisher 1995) following from the fact that the relationship between contiguous grey-values usually implies change. It is the manner that grey-values switch to their neighbors and weighs the overall activity level of image.

$$G = \left| \frac{\partial I}{\partial m} + \frac{\partial I}{\partial n} \right| \tag{9}$$

m and n denote the row and column of the image I.

5. Contrast: Contrast (C) is another ratio of the difference between the grey-values of the current pixel and the background to μ_I for magnifying the maximum likelihood of variation-dependent identification. Between the contrast and the visibility of an image, a high correlation exists (Li *et al.* 2002).

$$C = \left| \frac{I - \mu_I}{\mu_I} \right| \tag{10}$$

6. Definition: In order to find out where is how change, definition (*D*) is defined with the minimum m_i of all grey-values, the current grey-value, and the total deflection δ_I. Definition predicates that the more abrupt the change is, the clearer the feature of the image becomes.

$$D = \left| \frac{I - m_i}{\delta_I} \right| \tag{11}$$

$$\delta_I^2 = \frac{1}{MN} \sum_{x=0}^{M-1} \sum_{y=0}^{N-1} (I(x, y - m_i)^2 \tag{12}$$

7. Curvature: Curvature (*U*) is a ruler of the deflection extent, and it is rewarded by increasing the accuracy of smoothness or roughness recognition; on the other hand, it is an indicator of salient information that will actually guide the variation finder (Chakraborty *et al.* 1995).

$$U = \left| \frac{I - m_i}{m_a - m_i} \right| \tag{13}$$

m_a is the maximum grey-value.

Apparently, all features are cognate with each other, in other words, when one is high or goes down, so the others appear. Subsequently, a feature vector formed orderly from above seven features can be considered as a paradigm in a mathematical structure called feature space. It is evident that this representation space is beneficial to image processing and analysis technologies at heightening the precision of significance verdict in manner of replacing the original image with the feature vector as follows:

$$I_0 = \left[S\ V\ F\ G\ C\ D\ U \right] \tag{14}$$

2.2. Multivalued wavelet transform

The multivalued wavelet transform (MWT) employed can be performed by applying the RWT to each feature of I_0 as

$$\begin{aligned} I'_{j\text{-}1}(x,y) &= \sum_n h(n) I_{j-1}(x+n2^{j\text{-}1}, y) \\ I_j(x,y) &= \sum_n h(n) I'_{j\text{-}1}(x, y+n2^{j\text{-}1}) \\ \omega_j(x,y) &= I_{j-1}(x,y) - I_j(x,y);\ j = 1,\cdots,J \end{aligned} \tag{15}$$

The original feature vector I_0 can be rebuilt perfectly as

$$I_0(x,y) = I_J(x,y) + \sum_{j=1}^{J} \omega_j(x,y) \tag{16}$$

For fusing one multispectral (T) image and one panchromatic (P) image, the T image is first resampled to the pixel size of the P image. This fuser that produces the fused image (F) is summarized as follows:

$$\omega_{F_i}^j(x,y) = \begin{cases} \omega_{P_i}^j(x,y) & E(x,y) > 0 \\ \omega_{T_i}^j(x,y) & E(x,y) < 0 \\ (\omega_{P_i}^j(x,y) + \omega_{T_i}^j(x,y))/2 & E(x,y) = 0 \end{cases} \tag{17}$$

where $E(x, y)$ denotes the value of the electing map at position (x, y), and j is the decomposition level.

3. Example

3.1. Fusing QuickBird images using à trous wavelet

The raw images are downloaded from http://studio.gge.unb.ca/UNB/images. These images are acquired by a commercial satellite, QuickBird, which collects one 0.7 m resolution panchromatic band (450-900 nm) and blue (450-520 nm), green (520-600 nm), red (630-690 nm), near infrared (760-900 nm) bands of 2.8 m resolution. The QuickBird data set was taken over the Pyramid area of Egypt in 2002. The test images of size 1024 by 1024 at the resolution of 0.7 m are cut from the raw images and used as HRPI and LRMIs. Fig. 1(a) displays the LRMIs as a color composite where the red, green, blue bands are mapped into the RGB color space. The HRPI is shown in Fig. 1(b). The near infrared band is not shown because of the limited space

http://dx.doi.org/10.5772/56947

in this paper, although the images were processed and numerically evaluated. The study area is composed of various features such as roads, buildings, trees, etc., ranging in size from less than 5 m up to 50 m. It is obvious that the HRPI has better spatial resolution than the LRMIs and more details can be found from the HRPI. Before the image fusion, the raw LRMIs were resampled to the same pixel size of the HRPI in order to perform image registration.

The resolution ratio between the QuickBird HRPI and the LRMIs is 1: 4. Therefore, when performing the à trous based fusion algorithm, à trous filter $2^{-1/2}$(1/16, 1/4, 3/8, 1/4, 1/16), together with a decomposition level of two, is employed to abstract the high frequency information of the HRPI. Fused images are shown in Fig. 1(c).

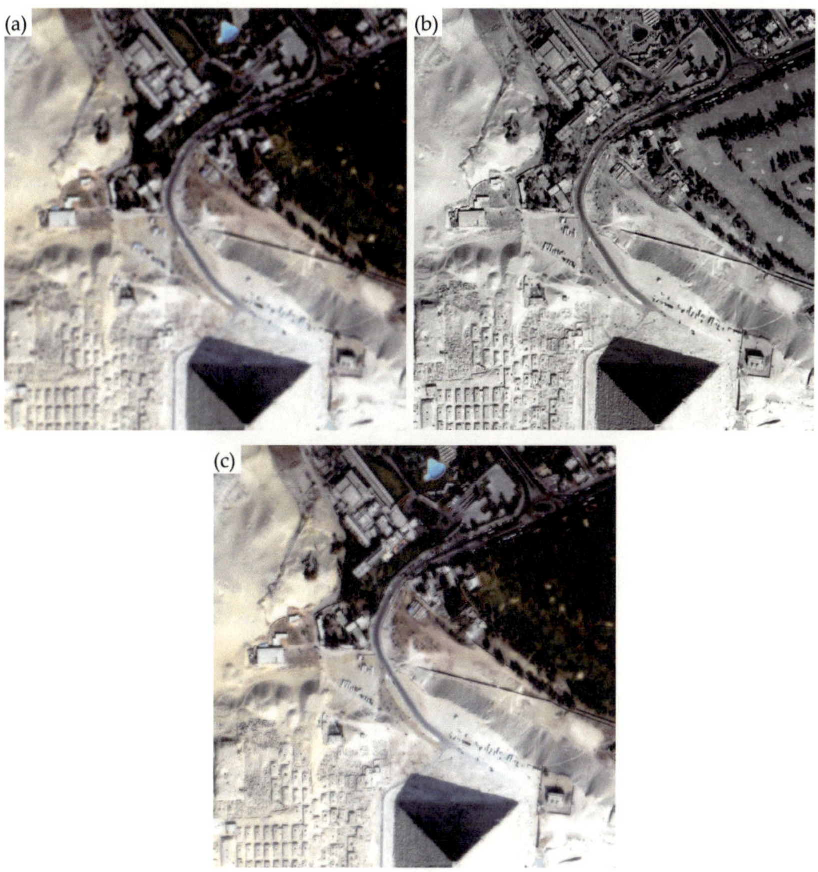

Figure 1. (a) the original LRMIs at 2.8 m resolution level; (b) the HRPI at 0.7 m resolution level; (c) the HRMIs produced from the AWT method

Visual inspection provides a comprehensive impression of image clarity and the similarity of the original and fused images (Wang et al., 2005). By visually comparing all the HRMIs (Fig. 1(c)) with the LRMI (Fig. 1(a)), it is apparent that the spatial resolutions of the HRMIs are much higher than that of the LRMI. Some small spatial structure details, such as edges, lines, which are not discernible in the LRMI, can be identified individually in each of the HRMIs. Buildings corners, holes, and textures are much sharper in Fig. 1(c) than in Fig. 1(a) and can be seen as clear as in Fig. 1(b). This means that the fusion method can improve the spatial quality of the LRMI during the fusion process.

3.2. Fusing TM and SPOT images using multivalued wavelet transform

In this section, three TM images (TM3=Red, TM4=near Infrared, TM5=Infrared) with 171×171 pixels and one SPOT image with 5120×5120 m^2 are fused using the MWT. For the MWT fuser, the three TM images are interpolated to 10 m pixel size in advance, the SPOT image, the TM image and their feature sequences are decomposed with RWT into three levels, and then the voting and electing fuser is fulfilled from the first to the third level. Figure 2(a), 2(b), and 2(c) exhibit the original TM image as a colour composite where TM3, TM4 and TM5 are coded in blue, green and red, the SPOT image, the fused image, respectively.

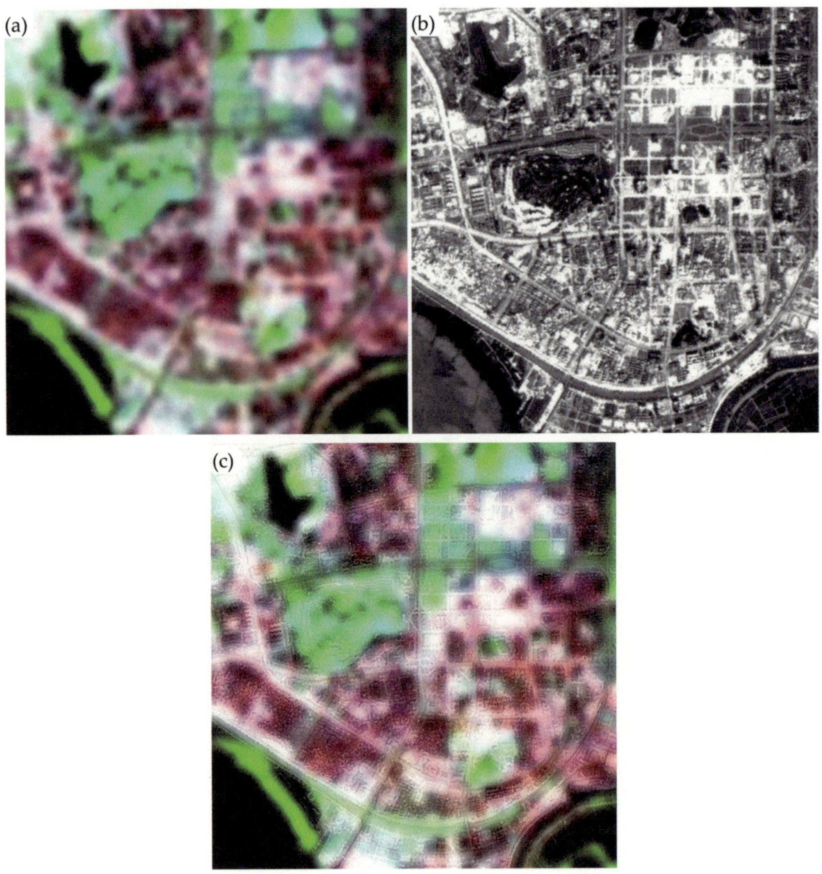

Figure 2. (a) The original TM images at 30 m resolution. (b) The SPOT image at 10 m resolution. (c) The fused images at 10 m resolution.

http://dx.doi.org/10.5772/56947

Compared visually with the original TM image, the spatial discernment of the fused images for the pair of fusers is undoubtedly better. Some small features, such as edges and lines, which are not interpretable in the original TM image can be identified individually in the fused images. Other large features, such as lakes, rivers and blocks, are much sharper than those in the original TM image. These signify that the fuser can assimilate spatial information from the SPOT image. Figure 2(c) shows less retained colours than figure 2(d), and recovery of the original colours is necessary for correct thematic mapping (Chibani and Houacine 2002). For instance, in figure 2(c), all of the green colours shown in the lower left part of figure 2(a) disappear. Second, with regard to clarity, a field of 'spider-web' shape in the left-of-centre part of figure 2(c) displays a 'salt-and-granule' face.

Author details

Shaohui Chen*

Address all correspondence to: chensh@igsnrr.ac.cn

Institute of Geographic Sciences and Natural Resources Research, Chinese Academy of Sciences, Beijing, China

References

[1] Chakraborty, A., Worring, M., and Duncan, J. S., 1995, On multi-feature integration for deformable boundary finding. Proceedings of the Fifth International Conference on Computer Vision, Cambridge, MA, USA, 20-23 June 1995 (Washington: IEEE Computer Society Publications), 846-851.

[2] Chen, S. H., Su, H. B. and Zhang, R. H., 2008, Feature space and measure metric for fusing multisensor images. International Journal of Remote Sensing, 29, 3257–3270.

[3] Chen S. H., Su H. B., Zhang R. H., Tian J., 2008, Fusing remote sensing images using a` trous wavelet transform and empirical mode decomposition. Pattern Recognition Letters 29, 330–342.

[4] Chibani, Y., and Houacine, A., 2002, the joint use of IHS transform and redundant wavelet decomposition for fusing multispectral and panchromatic images. International Journal of Remote Sensing, 23, 3821-3833.

[5] Chibani, Y., Houacine, A., 2003, Redundant versus orthogonal wavelet decomposition for multisensor image fusion. Pattern Recognition 36, 879-887.

[6] Eskicioglu, A. M., and Fisher, P. S., 1995, Image quality measures and their performance. IEEE Transactions on Communications, 43, 2959-2965.

[7] Garzelli, A., 2002, Possibilities and limitations of the use of wavelets in image fusion. In Proceedings of IEEE International Geoscience and Remote Sensing Symposium, 24-28 June 2002, Toronto, Ontario, Canada (Washington: IEEE Inc.), 1, pp. 66–68.

[8] Li, S. T., Kwok, J. T., and Wang, Y. N., 2002, Multifocus image fusion using artificial neural networks. Pattern Recognition Letters, 23, 985-997.

[9] Liu, J. G., 2000, Smoothing filter-based intensity modulation: a spectral preserve image fusion technique for improving spatial details. International Journal of Remote Sensing, 21, 3461-3472.

[10] Liu, Y. X., and Li, Y. D., 1997, New approaches of multifractal image analysis. Proceedings of International Conference on Information, Communications and Signal Processing, Singapore, 9-12 Sept. 1997 (New York: IEEE Publications), 2, 970-974.

[11] Lu, J., and Healy, JR., D. M., 1994, Contrast enhancement via multiscale gradient transformation. Proceedings of IEEE International Conference on Image processing, Texas, USA, 13-16 Nov. 1994 (CA, USA: IEEE Computer Society Publications), 2, 482-486.

[12] Mallat, S. G., and Zhong, S., 1992, Characterization of signals from multiscale edges. *IEEE Transaction Pattern Anaysis Machine Intelligence*, 14, 710-732.

[13] Nikolov, S. G., Bull, D. R., and Canagarajah, C. N., 2000, 2-D image fusion by multiscale edge graph combination. Proceedings of the Third International Conference on Information Fusion, Paris, France, 10-13 July 2000 (CA, USA: International Society of Information Fusion Publications), 1, MOD3/16- MOD3/22.

[14] Núñez J., Otazu, X., et al., 1999, Multiresolution-based image fusion with additive wavelet decomposition, IEEE Transactions on Geoscience and Remote Sensing, vol. 37, no. 3, 1204-1211.

[15] Wang, Z. J., Ziou, D., Armenakis, C., Li, D. R., and Li, Q. Q., 2005, A comparative analysis of image fusion methods. IEEE Transactions on Geoscience and Remote Sensing, 43, 1391-1402.

Chapter 7

Image Fusion Based on Shearlets

Miao Qiguang, Shi Cheng and Li Weisheng

Additional information is available at the end of the chapter

http://dx.doi.org/10.5772/56945

1. Introduction

Image decomposition is important to image fusion and affects the information extraction quality, even the whole fusion quality. Wavelet theory has been developed since the beginning of the last century. It was first applied to signal processing in the 1980's[1], and over the past decade it has been recognized as having great potential in image processing applications, as well as in image fusion[2]. Wavelet transforms are more useful than Fourier transforms, and it is efficient in dealing with one-dimensional point-wise smooth signal [3-5]. However the limitations of the direction make it not perform well for multidimensional data. Images contain sharp transition such as edges, and wavelet transforms are not optimally efficient in representing them.

Recently, a theory for multidimensional data called multi-scale geometric analysis (MGA) has been developed. Many MGA tools were proposed, such as ridgelet, curvelet, bandelet, contourlet, etc [6-9]. The new MGA tools provide higher directional sensitivity than wavelets. Shearlets, a new approach provided in 2005, possess not only all above properties, but equipped with a rich mathematical structure similar to wavelets, which are associated to a multiresolution analysis. The shearlets form a tight frame at various scales and directions, and are optimally sparse in representing images with edges. Only the curvelets has the similar properties with shearlets [10-14]. But the construction of curvelets is not built directly in the discrete domain and it does not provide a multiresolution representation of the geometry. The decomposition of shearlets is similar to contourlets, while the contourlet transform consists of an application of the Laplacian pyramid followed by directional filtering, for shearlets, the directional filtering is replaced by a shear matrix. An important advantage of the shearlet transform over the contourlet transform is that there are no restrictions on the direction numbers. [15-19]

In recent years, the theory of the shearlets, which is used in image processing, has been studied gradually. Now the applications of shearlets are mainly in image denoising, sparse image representation [20] and edge detection [21, 22]. Its applications in image fusion are still under exploring.

2. Shearlets [12, 20]

2.1. The theory of Shearlets

In dimension $n=2$, the affine systems with composite dilations are defined as follows.

$$A_{AS}(\psi)=\{\psi_{j,l,k}(x)=|\det A|^{j/2}\,\psi(S^l A^j x-k): j,l\in ¢, k\in ¢^2\} \tag{1}$$

Where $\psi\in L^2(\mathbb{R}^2)$, A, S are both 2×2 invertible matrices, and $|\det S|=1$, the elements of this system are called composite wavelet if $A_{AS}(\psi)$ forms a tight frame for $L^2(\mathbb{R}^2)$.

$$\sum_{j,l,k}|<f,\psi_{j,l,k}>|^2=\|f\|^2$$

Let A denote the parabolic scaling matrix and S denote the shear matrix. For each $a>0$ and $s\in\mathbb{R}$,

$$A=\begin{pmatrix}a & 0\\ 0 & \sqrt{a}\end{pmatrix}, S=\begin{pmatrix}1 & s\\ 0 & 1\end{pmatrix}.$$

The matrices described above have the special roles in shearlet transform. The first matrix $\begin{pmatrix}a & 0\\ 0 & \sqrt{a}\end{pmatrix}$ controls the 'scale' of the shearlets, by applying a fine dilation faction along the two axes, which ensures that the frequency support of the shearlets becomes increasingly elongated at finer scales. The second matrix $\begin{pmatrix}1 & s\\ 0 & 1\end{pmatrix}$, on the other hand, is not expansive, and only controls the orientation of the shearlets. The size of frequency support of the shearlets is illustrated in Fig. 1 for some particular values of a and s.

$\psi_{j,l,k}$ for different values of a and s.

In references [12], assume $a=4$, $s=1$, where $A=A_0$ is the anisotropic dilation matrix and $S=S_0$ is the shear matrix, which are given by

$$A_0=\begin{pmatrix}4 & 0\\ 0 & 2\end{pmatrix}, \quad S_0=\begin{pmatrix}1 & 1\\ 0 & 1\end{pmatrix}$$

For $\forall\,\xi=(\xi_1,\xi_2)\in\hat{\mathbb{R}}^2$, $\xi_1\neq0$, let $\hat{\psi}^{(0)}(\xi)$ be given by

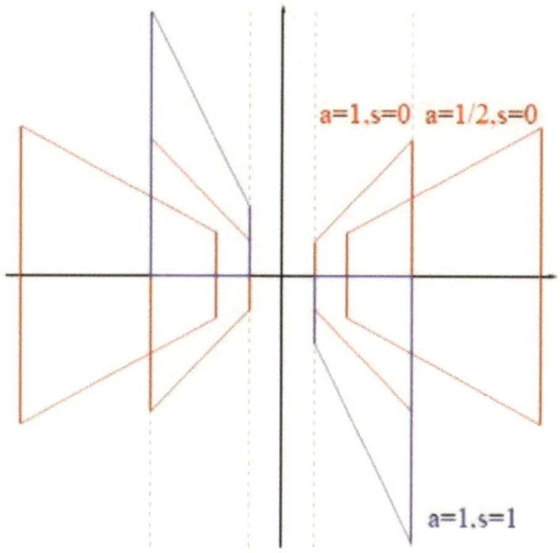

Figure 1. frequency support of the shearlets

$$\hat{\psi}^{(0)}(\xi)=\hat{\psi}^{(0)}(\xi_1,\xi_2)=\hat{\psi}_1(\xi_1)\hat{\psi}_2(\frac{\xi_2}{\xi_1}) \tag{2}$$

Where $\hat{\psi}_1 \in C^{\infty}(\mathbb{R})$ is a wavelet, and $\mathrm{supp}\hat{\psi}_1 \subset [-1/2,\ -1/16] \cup [1/16,\ 1/2]$; $\hat{\psi}_2 \in C^{\infty}(\mathbb{R})$, and $\mathrm{supp}\hat{\psi}_2 \subset [-1,1]$. This implies $\hat{\psi}^{(0)} \in C^{\infty}(\mathbb{R})$, and $\mathrm{supp}\hat{\psi}^{(0)} \subset [-1/2,\ 1/2]^2$.

In addition, we assume that

$$\sum_{j\geq 0}|\hat{\psi}_1(2^{-2j}\omega)|^2=1, \qquad |\omega|\geq 1/8 \tag{3}$$

and for $\forall\ j\geq 0$

$$\sum_{l=-2^j}^{2^j-1}|\hat{\psi}_2(2^j\omega-l)|^2=1, \qquad |\omega|\leq 1 \tag{4}$$

There are several examples of functions ψ_1, ψ_2 satisfying the properties described above. Eq. (3) and (4) imply that

$$\sum_{j\geq 0}\sum_{l=-2^j}^{2^j-1}|\hat{\psi}^{(0)}(\xi A_0^{-j}S_0^{-l})|^2=\sum_{j\geq 0}\sum_{l=-2^j}^{2^j-1}|\hat{\psi}_1(2^{-2j}\xi_1)|^2|\hat{\psi}_2(2^j\frac{\xi_2}{\xi_1}-l)|^2=1, \tag{5}$$

for any $(\xi_1, \xi_2) \in D_0$, where $D_0 = \{(\xi_1, \xi_2) \in \hat{\mathbb{R}}^2 : |\xi_1| \geq 1/8, |\xi_2| \leq 1\}$, the functions $\{\hat{\psi}^{(0)}(\xi A_0^{-j} S_0^{-l})\}$ form a tiling of D_0. This is illustrated in Fig.2 (a). This property described above implies that the collection

$$\{\psi_{j,l,k}^{(0)}(x) = 2^{\frac{3j}{2}} \psi^{(0)}(S_0^l A_0^j x - k) : j \geq 0, -2^j \leq l \leq 2^j - 1, k \in ¢^2\} \tag{6}$$

is a Parseval frame for $L^2(D_0)^\vee = \{f \in L^2(\mathbb{R}^2) : \text{supp}\, \hat{f} \subset D_0\}$. And from the conditions on the support of $\hat{\psi}_1$ and $\hat{\psi}_2$ one can easily observe that the function $\psi_{j,l,k}$ have frequency support,

$$\text{supp}\, \hat{\psi}_{j,k,l}^{(0)} \subset \{(\xi_1, \xi_2) : \xi_1 \in [-2^{2j-1}, -2^{2j-4}] \cup [2^{2j-4}, 2^{2j-1}], |\frac{\xi_2}{\xi_1} + l2^{-j}| \leq 2^{-j}\} \tag{7}$$

That is, each element $\hat{\psi}_{j,l,k}$ is support on a pair of trapezoids, of approximate size $2^{2j} \times 2^j$, oriented along lines of slope $l2^{-j}$.(see Fig.2 (b)).

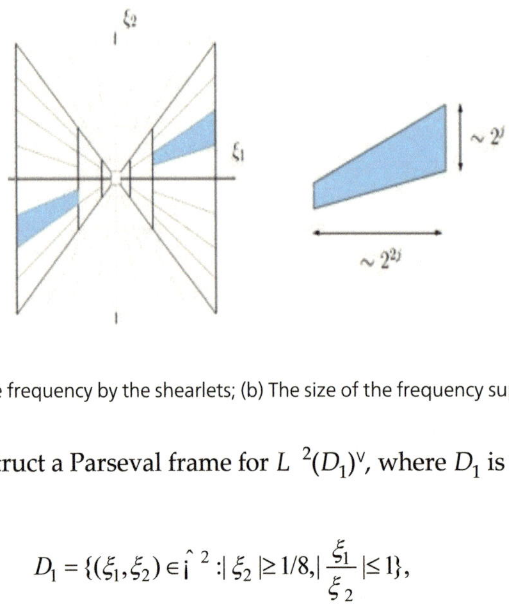

Figure 2. (a) The tiling of the frequency by the shearlets; (b) The size of the frequency support of a shearlet $\psi_{j,l,k}$.

Similarly we can construct a Parseval frame for $L^2(D_1)^\vee$, where D_1 is the vertical cone,

$$D_1 = \{(\xi_1, \xi_2) \in \hat{¡}^2 : |\xi_2| \geq 1/8, |\frac{\xi_1}{\xi_2}| \leq 1\}, \tag{8}$$

Let

$$A_1 = \begin{pmatrix} 2 & 0 \\ 0 & 4 \end{pmatrix}, \quad S_1 = \begin{pmatrix} 1 & 0 \\ 1 & 1 \end{pmatrix}$$

and $\hat{\psi}^{(1)}(\xi)=\hat{\psi}^{(1)}(\xi_1, \xi_2)=\hat{\psi}_1(\xi_2)\hat{\psi}_2(\frac{\xi_1}{\xi_2})$, where $\hat{\psi}_1$ and $\hat{\psi}_2$ are defined as (2) and (3), then the Parseval frame for $L^2(D_1)^{\vee}$ is as follows,

$$\{\psi_{j,l,k}^{(1)}(x) = 2^{\frac{3j}{2}} \psi^{(1)}(S_1^l A_1^j x - k) : j \geq 0, -2^j \leq l \leq 2^j - 1, k \in ¢^2\}. \tag{9}$$

To make this discussion more rigorous, it will be useful to examine this problem from the point of view of approximation theory. If $F=\{\psi_\mu : \mu \in I\}$ is a bas is or, more generally, a tight frame for $L^2(R^2)$, then an image f can be approximated by the partial sums

$$f_M = \sum_{\mu \in I_M} < f, \psi_\mu > \psi_\mu, \tag{10}$$

Where I_M is the index set of the M largest inner products $| < f, \psi_\mu > |$. The resulting approximation error is

$$\varepsilon_M = \| f - f_M \|^2 = \sum_{\mu \notin I_M} | f, \psi_\mu |^2, \tag{11}$$

and this quantity approaches asymptotically zero as M increases.

The approximation error of Fourier approximations is $\varepsilon_M \leq CM^{-1/2}$, of the Wavelet is $\varepsilon_M \leq CM^{-1}$, and the approximation error of Shearlets is $\varepsilon_M \leq C(\log M)^3 M^{-2}$, which is better than Fourier and Wavelet approximations.

2.2. Discrete Shearlets

It will be convenient to describe the collection of shearlets presented above in a way which is more suitable to derive numerical implementation. For $\xi=(\xi_1, \xi_2) \in \hat{R}^2$, $j \geq 0$ and $l=-2^j, \cdots, 2^j-1$, Let

$$W_{j,l}^0(\xi) = \begin{cases} \hat{\psi}_2(2^j \frac{\xi_2}{\xi_1} - l)\chi_{D_0}(\xi) + \hat{\psi}_2(2^j \frac{\xi_1}{\xi_2} - l + 1)\chi_{D_1}(\xi) & l = -2^j \\ \hat{\psi}_2(2^j \frac{\xi_2}{\xi_1} - l)\chi_{D_0}(\xi) + \hat{\psi}_2(2^j \frac{\xi_1}{\xi_2} - l\text{-}1)\chi_{D_1}(\xi) & l = 2^j - 1 \\ \hat{\psi}_2(2^j \frac{\xi_2}{\xi_1} - l) & otherwise \end{cases} \tag{12}$$

and

$$W_{j,l}^{1}(\xi)=\begin{cases}\hat{\psi}_2(2^j\frac{\xi_2}{\xi_1}-l+1)\chi_{D_0}(\xi)+\hat{\psi}_2(2^j\frac{\xi_1}{\xi_2}-l)\chi_{D_1}(\xi) & l=-2^j\\ \hat{\psi}_2(2^j\frac{\xi_2}{\xi_1}-l-1)\chi_{D_0}(\xi)+\hat{\psi}_2(2^j\frac{\xi_1}{\xi_2}-l)\chi_{D_1}(\xi) & l=2^j-1\\ \hat{\psi}_2(2^j\frac{\xi_1}{\xi_2}-l) & otherwise\end{cases} \tag{13}$$

Where ψ_2, D_0, D_1 are defined in section 2. For $-2^j \le l \le 2^j-2$, each term $W_{j,l}^{(d)}(\xi)$ is a window function localized on a pair of trapezoids, as illustrated in fig.1a. When $l=-2^j$ or $l=2^j-1$, at the junction of the horizontal cone D_0 and the vertical cone, $W_{j,l}^{(d)}(\xi)$ is the superposition of two such function.

Using this notation, for $j\ge 0$, $-2^j+1\le l\le 2^j-2$, $k\in Z^2$, $d=0$, 1, we can write the Fourier transform of the Shearlets in the compact form

$$\hat{\psi}_{j,l,k}^{(d)}(\xi)=2^{\frac{3j}{2}}V(2^{-2j}\xi)W_{j,l}^{(d)}(\xi)e^{-2\pi i\xi A_d^{-j}B_d^{-l}k} \tag{14}$$

Where $V(\xi_1, \xi_2)=\hat{\psi}_1(\xi_1)\chi_{D_0}(\xi_1, \xi_2)+\hat{\psi}_1(\xi_2)\chi_{D_1}(\xi_1, \xi_2)$.

The Shearlet transform of $f\in L^2(R^2)$ can be computed by

$$< f,\psi_{j,l,k}^{(d)} >=2^{\frac{3j}{2}}\int_{R^2}\hat{f}(\xi)\overline{V(2^{-2j}\xi)W_{j,l}^{(d)}(\xi)}e^{-2\pi i\xi A_d^{-j}B_d^{-l}k}d\xi \tag{15}$$

Indeed, one can easily verify that

$$\sum_{d=0}^{1}\sum_{l=-2^j}^{2^j-1}|W_{j,l}^{(d)}(\xi_1,\xi_2)|^2=1 \tag{16}$$

And form this it follows that

$$|\hat{\phi}(\xi_1,\xi_2)|^2+\sum_{d=0}^{1}\sum_{j\ge 0}\sum_{l=-2^j}^{2^j-1}|V(2^{2j}\xi_1,2^{2j}\xi_2)||W_{j,l}^{(d)}(\xi_1,\xi_2)|^2=1 \tag{17}$$

http://dx.doi.org/10.5772/56945

3. Multi-focus image fusion based on Shearlets

3.1. Algorithm framework of multi-focus image fusion using Shearlets

3.1.1. Image decomposition

Image decomposition based on shearlet transform is composed by two parts, decomposition of multi-direction and multi-scale.

1. Multi-direction decomposition of image using shear matrix S_0 or S_1.

2. Multi-scale decompose of each direction using wavelet packets decomposition.

In step (1), if the image is decomposed only by S_0, or by S_1, the number of the directions is $2(l+1)+1$. If the image is decomposed both by S_0 and S_1, the number of the directions is $2(l+2)+2$. The framework of Image decomposition with shearlets is shown in Fig. 3.

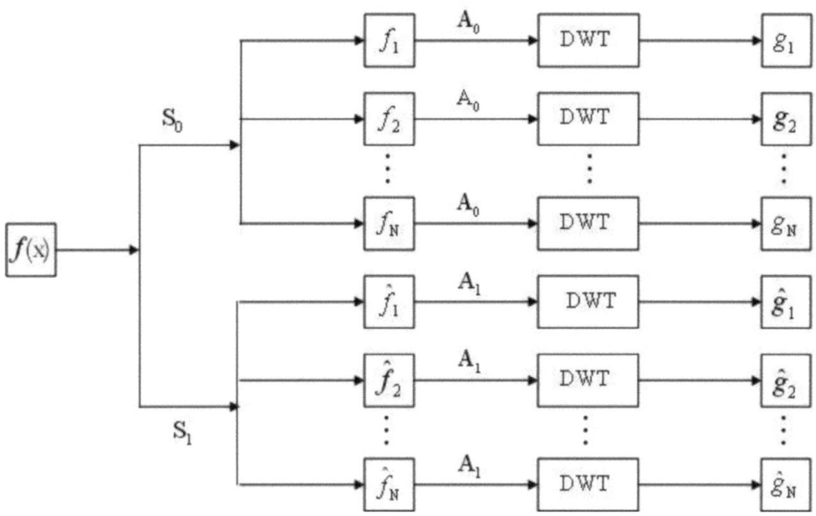

Figure 3. Image decomposition framework with shearlets

3.1.2. Image fusion

Image fusion framework based on shearlets is shown in Fig. 4. The following steps of image fusion are adopted.

1. The two images taking part in the fusion are geometrically reg is tered to each other.

2. Transform the original images using shearlets. Both horizontal and vertical cones are adopted in this method. The number of the directions is 6. Then the wavelet packets are used in multi-scale decomposition with $j=5$.

3. Fusion rule based on regional absolute value is adopted in this algorithem.

a. The choice of low frequency coefficients.

Low frequency coefficients of the fused image are replaced by the average of low frequency coefficients of the two source images.

b. The choice of high frequency coefficients.

$$D_X(i,j) = \sum_{i \le M, j \le N} |Y_X(i,j)|, \quad X = A,B \tag{18}$$

Calculate the absolute value of high frequency coefficients in the neighborhood by Eq.(18) Where $M = N = 3$ is the size of the neighborhood, X denotes the two source images, $D_X(i, j)$ is the regional absolute value of X image within 3 neighborhood with the center at (i, j), $Y_X(i, j)$ means the pixel value at (i, j) from X.

Select the high frequency coefficients from the two source images.

$$F(i,j) = \begin{cases} A(i,j) & D_A(i,j) \ge D_B(i,j) \\ B(i,j) & D_A(i,j) < D_B(i,j) \end{cases} \tag{19}$$

Where F is the high frequency coefficients of the fused image.

Finally the region consistency check is done based on the fuse-decision map, which is shown in Eq.(20).

$$Map(i,j) = \begin{cases} 1 & D_A(i,j) \ge D_B(i,j) \\ 0 & D_A(i,j) < D_B(i,j) \end{cases} \tag{20}$$

According to Eq.(20), if the certain coefficient in the fused image is to come from source image A, but with the majority of its surrounding neighbors from B, this coefficient will be switched to come from B.

4. The fused image is gotten using the inverse shearlet transform.

3.2. Simulation experiments

1. Multi-focus image of Bottle

The following group images are selected to prove the validity proposed in this section.

The two source images, Fig.5.(a) and (b), are the multi-focus images, which focus on the different parts. The fusion methods of these experiments are shearlets, contourlets, Haar, Daubechies, PCA and Laplacian Pyramid (LP). Fusion rule mentioned above is used in this

http://dx.doi.org/10.5772/56945

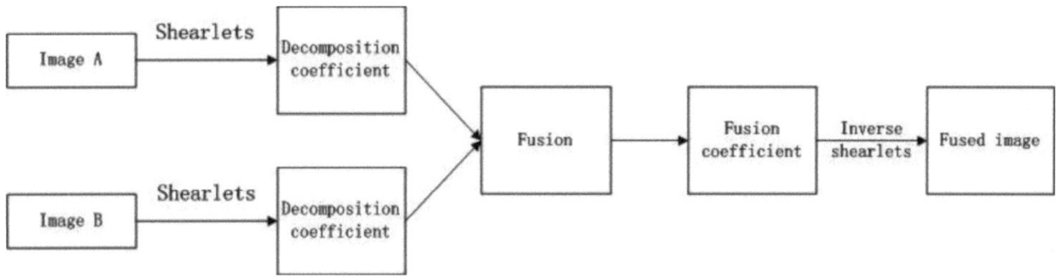

Figure 4. Image fusion framework based on shearlets

experiment. The following image quality metrics are used in this experiment: Standard deviation (STD), Difference of entropy (DEN), Overall cross entropy (OCE), Entropy (EN), Sharpness (SP), Peak signal to noise ratio (PSNR), Mean square error (MSE) and Q.

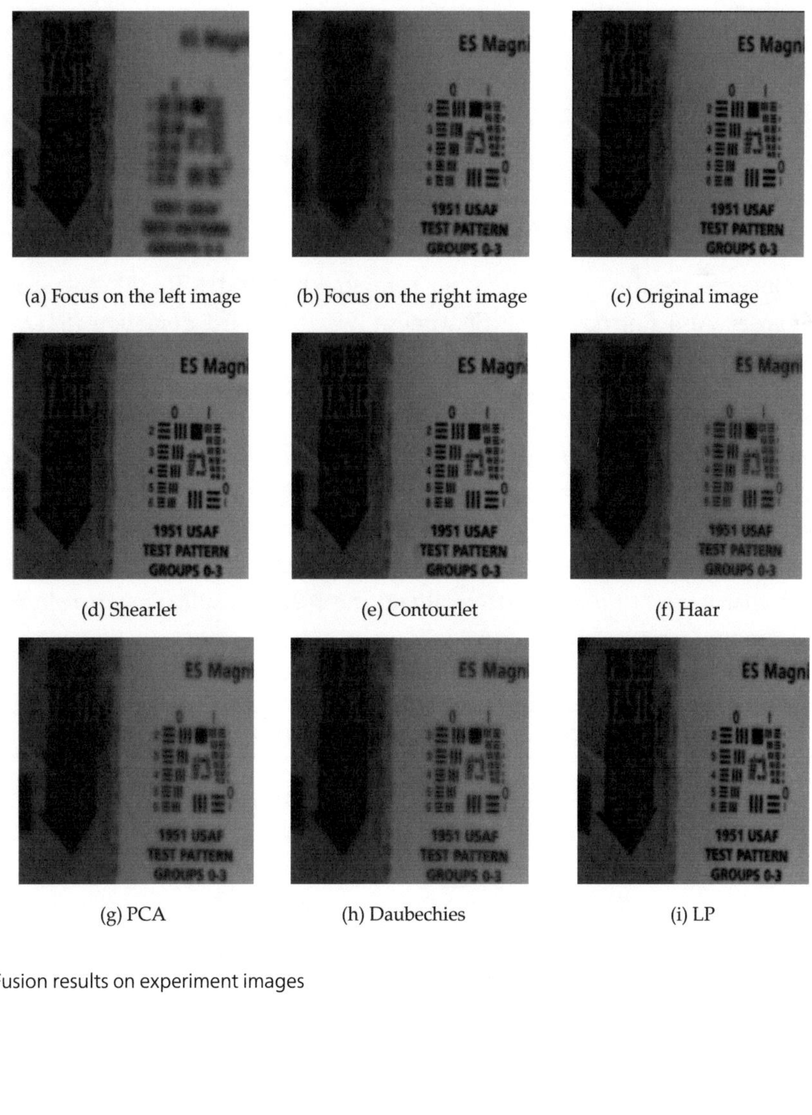

(a) Focus on the left image (b) Focus on the right image (c) Original image

(d) Shearlet (e) Contourlet (f) Haar

(g) PCA (h) Daubechies (i) LP

Figure 5. Fusion results on experiment images

Fig.5. (c) is the ideal image, Fig.5.(d) ~Fig.5.(i) are the fused images with different methods. From the subjective evaluation of Fig.6 and objective metrics from Table 1, we can see that shearlet transform have more detail information, disperse the gray level and higher sharpness of the fused image than other methods do.

	shearlet	contourlet	Haar	Daubechies	PCA	LP
STD	43.3322	43.3313	41.3589	41.2225	41.3253	44.1356
DEN	0.0021	0.0227	0.0150	0.0144	0.0113	0.0354
OCE	0.0107	0.0125	0.0442	0.0470	0.0484	0.0179
EN	6.9628	6.9577	6.9499	6.9493	6.9462	6.9703
SP	19.1502	18.7049	15.3007	14.8401	12.9532	19.4853
PSNR	40.8004	39.3935	31.4881	31.188	31.1887	40.3666
MSE	5.0067	7.0625	45.8016	49.0528	49.4549	5.9761
Q	0.9042	0.8703	0.8954	0.9010	0.9131	0.8809

Table 1. Comparison of multi-focus image fusion

2. Multi-focus Images of CT and MRI

The source images are the CT (Computer Tomography) and MRI (Magnetic Resonance Imaging) images. And Entropy (EN), Sharpness (SP), Standard deviation (STD) and Q is used to evaluate the effect of the fused images.

Fig.6 (a) is a CT image, whose brightness has relation with tissue density and the bone is shown clearly, but soft tissue is invisible. Fig.6 (b) is a MRI image, whose brightness has relation with the number of hydrogen atoms in t issue, so the soft t issue is shown clearly, but the bone is invisible. The CT image and the MRI image are complementary, the advantages could be fused into one image. The desired standard image cannot be acquired, thus only entropy and sharpness are adopted to evaluate the fusion result. Fusion rule mentioned above is used in this experiment.

	Shearlet	Contourlet	Haar	Daubechies	PCA	Average
EN	6.1851	5.9189	5.9870	5.9784	5.8792	5.9868
SP	20.5271	24.8884	16.9938	14.8810	17.2292	16.9935
STD	45.0704	50.4706	35.8754	35.1490	45.3889	34.9141
Q	0.6881	0.3022	0.4960	0.4994	0.6847	0.4943

Table 2. Comparison of medical image fusion

http://dx.doi.org/10.5772/56945

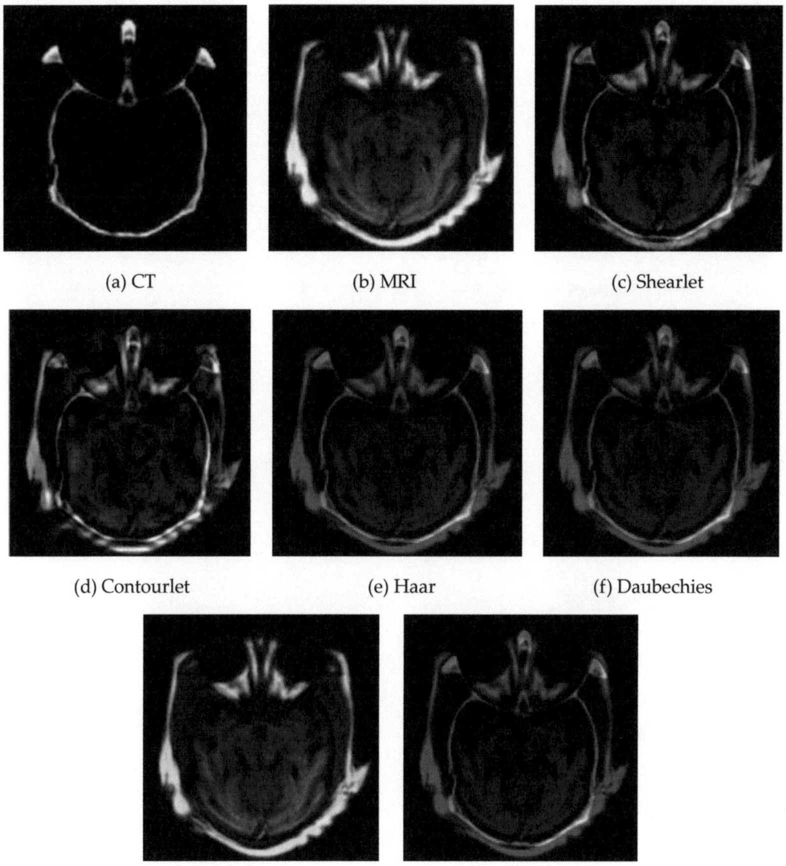

(a) CT (b) MRI (c) Shearlet

(d) Contourlet (e) Haar (f) Daubechies

(g) PCA (h) Average

Figure 6. Fusion results on experiment images

4. Remote sensing image fusion based on Shearlets and PCNN

4.1. Theory of PCNN

PCNN, called the third generation artificial neural network, is feedback network formed by the connection of lots of neurons, according to the inspiration of biologic v is ual cortex pattern. Every neuron is made up of three sections: receptive section, modulation and pulse generator section, which can be described by discrete equation [23-25].

The receptive field receives the input from the other neurons or external environment, and transmits them in two channels: F-channel and L -channel. In the modulation on field, add a positive offset on signal L_j from L -channel; use the result to multiply modulation with signal F_j from F-channel. When the neuron threshold $\theta_j \geq U_j$, the pulse generator is turned off; otherwise, the pulse generator is turned on, and output a pulse. The mathematic model of PCNN is described below [26-30].

$$\begin{cases} F_{ij}[n]=\exp(-\alpha_F)F_{ij}[n-1]+V_F\sum m_{ijkl}Y_{kl}[n-1]+S_{ij} \\ L_{ij}[n]=\exp(-\alpha_L)L_{ij}[n-1]+V_L\sum w_{ijkl}Y_{kl}[n-1] \\ U_{ij}[n]=F_{ij}[n](1+\beta L_{ij}[n]) \\ Y_{ij}[n]=1 \quad if\ U_{ij}[n]>\theta_{ij}[n]\ or\ 0\ otherwise \\ \theta_{ij}[n]=\exp(-\alpha_\theta)\theta_{ij}[n-1]+V_\theta Y_{ij}[n-1] \end{cases} \tag{21}$$

Where α_F, α_L is the constant time of decay, α_θ is the threshold constant time of decay, V_θ is the threshold amplitude coefficient, V_F, V_L are the link amplitude coefficients, β is the value of link strength, and m_{ijkl}, w_{ijkl} are the link weight matrix.

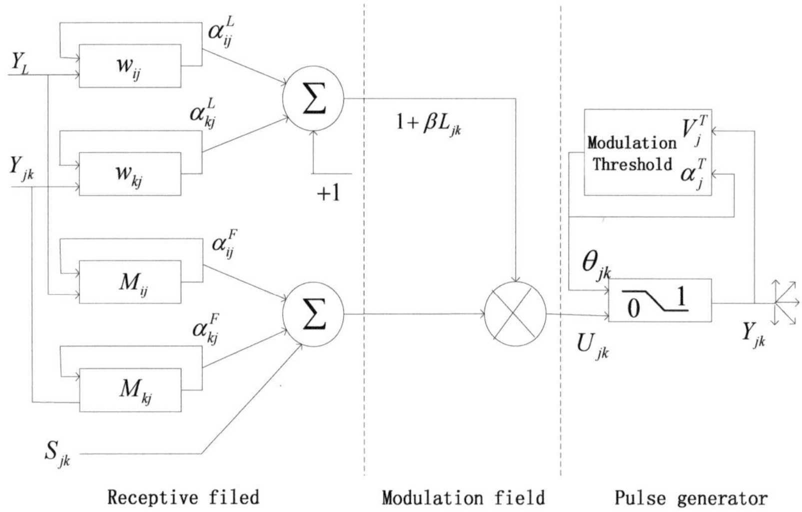

Figure 7. The model of PCNN neuron

4.2. Algorithm framework of remote sensing image fusion using Shearlts and PCNN

When PCNN is used for image processing, it is a single two-dimensional network. The number of the neurons is equal to the number of pixels. There is a one-to-one correspondence between the image pixels and the network neurons.

In this paper, Shearlets and PCNN are used to fuse images. The steps are described below:

1. Decompose the original images A and B respectively into many different directions f_{NA}, $\hat{f}_{NA}$, f_{NB}, $\hat{f}_{NB}$ ($N=1, ..., n$) via Shear matrixs (In this chapter, $n=3$).

2. Calculate the gradient features in every direction to form feature maps, $Grad\, f_{NA}$, $Grad\, \hat{f}_{NA}$, $Grad\, f_{NB}$, $Grad\, \hat{f}_{NB}$.

3. Decompose feature map of all directions using DWT, $DG f_{NA}$, $DG \hat{f}_{NA}$, $DG f_{NB} DG \hat{f}_{NB}$ are high frequency coefficients after the decomposition.

4. Take $DG f_{NA}$, $DG \hat{f}_{NA}$, $DG f_{NB} DG \hat{f}_{NB}$ into PCNN, and fire maps in all directions $fire\, f_{NA}$, $fire\, \hat{f}_{NA}$, $fire\, f_{NB}$, $fire\, \hat{f}_{NB}$ are obtained.

5. Take the Shearlets on original images A and B, the high frequency coefficients in all directions are f_{NA}^h, $\hat{f}_{NA}^h$, f_{NB}^h and $\hat{f}_{NB}^h$, and the low are f_{NA}^l, $\hat{f}_{NA}^l$, f_{NB}^l and $\hat{f}_{NB}^l$. The fused high frequency coefficients in all directions can be selected as follow:

$$f_N^h = \begin{cases} f_{NA}^h, & fire\, f_{NA} \geq fire\, f_{NB} \\ f_{NB}^h, & fire\, f_{NA} < fire\, f_{NB} \end{cases}, \qquad \hat{f}_N^h = \begin{cases} \hat{f}_{NA}^h, & fire\, \hat{f}_{NA} \geq fire\, \hat{f}_{NB} \\ \hat{f}_{NB}^h, & fire\, \hat{f}_{NA} < fire\, \hat{f}_{NB} \end{cases}.$$

The fusion rule of the low frequency coefficients in any direction is described below:

$$f_N^l = \begin{cases} f_{NA}^l, & Var\, f_{NA}^l \geq Var\, f_{NB}^l \\ f_{NB}^l, & Var\, f_{NA}^l < Var\, f_{NB}^l \end{cases}, \qquad \hat{f}_N^l = \begin{cases} \hat{f}_{NA}^l, & Var\, \hat{f}_{NA}^l \geq Var\, \hat{f}_{NB}^l \\ \hat{f}_{NB}^l, & Var\, \hat{f}_{NA}^l < Var\, \hat{f}_{NB}^l \end{cases}$$

Where $Varf$ is the variance of f.

6. The fused image is obtained using the inverse Shearlet transform.

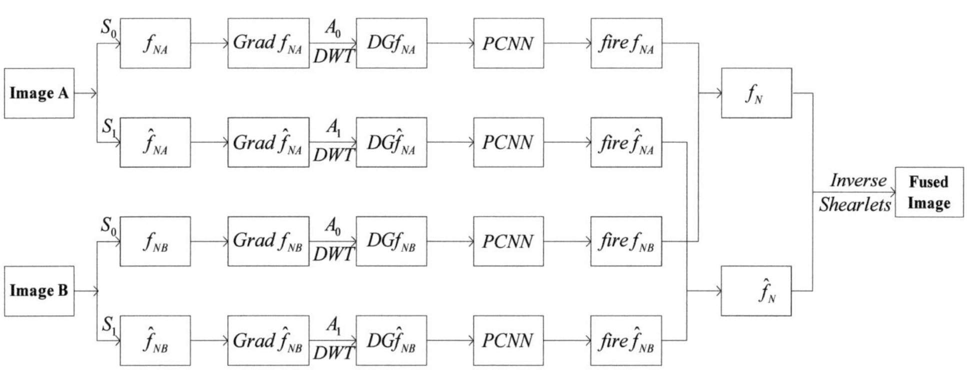

Figure 8. Image fusion framework with Shearlets and PCNN

4.3. Simulation experiments

In this section, three different examples, Optical and SAR images, remote sensing image and hyperspectral image, are provided to demonstrate the effectiveness of the proposed method. Many different methods, including Average, Laplacian Pyramid (LP), Gradient Pyramid (GP), Contrast Pyramid (CP), Contourlet-PCNN (C-P), and Wavelet-PCNN (W-P), are used to compare with our proposed approach. The subjective v is ual perception gives us direct Comparisons, and some objective image quality assessments are also used to evaluate the performance of the proposed approach. The following image quality metrics are used in this paper: Entropy (EN), Overall cross entropy (OCE), Standard deviation (STD), Average gradient (Ave-grad), Q, and $Q_{AB/F}$.

In these three different experiments, the parameters of values of PCNN are showing as follows:

Experiment 1: $\alpha_L = 0.03$, $\alpha_\theta = 0.1$, $V_L = 1$, $V_\theta = 10$, $\beta = 0.2$, $W = \begin{pmatrix} 1/\sqrt{2} & 1 & 1/\sqrt{2} \\ 1 & 1 & 1 \\ 1/\sqrt{2} & 1 & 1/\sqrt{2} \end{pmatrix}$, and the iterative number is $n = 100$.

Experiment 2: $\alpha_L = 0.02$, $\alpha_\theta = 0.05$, $V_L = 1$, $V_\theta = 15$, $\beta = 0.7$, $W = \begin{pmatrix} 1/\sqrt{2} & 1 & 1/\sqrt{2} \\ 1 & 1 & 1 \\ 1/\sqrt{2} & 1 & 1/\sqrt{2} \end{pmatrix}$, and the iterative number is $n = 100$.

Experiment 3: $\alpha_L = 0.03$, $\alpha_\theta = 0.1$, $V_L = 1$, $V_\theta = 15$, $\beta = 0.5$, $W = \begin{pmatrix} 1/\sqrt{2} & 1 & 1/\sqrt{2} \\ 1 & 1 & 1 \\ 1/\sqrt{2} & 1 & 1/\sqrt{2} \end{pmatrix}$, and the iterative number is $n = 100$.

As optical and SAR images, remote sensing image and hyperspectral image are widely used in military, so the study of these images in image fusion are of very important.

Fig.9-11 gives the fused images with Shearlet-PCNN and some other different methods. From Fig.9-11 and Table3, we can see that image fusion based on Shearlets and PCNN can get more information and less distortion than other methods. In experiment 1, the edge feature from Fig. 9(a) and spectral information from Fig. 9(b) are kept in the fused image by using the proposed method, which is showing in Fig.9(c). In Fig.9 (d), the spectral character in the fused image, fused by Contourlet and PCNN, is distorted and the from visual point of view, the color of image is too prominent. From Fig.9 (e)-(f), spectral information of the fused images is lost and the edge features are vague. Fig. 10 are the fused Remote sensing image, which is able to provide more new information since it can penetrate clouds, rain, and even vegetation. With different imaging modalities and different bands, its features are different in each image. In Fig.10(c) and (d), band 8 has more river characteristics but less city information, while band 4 has opposite imaging features.

Fig.10 (c) is the fused image using Shearlets and PCNN. The numerical results in Fig.5 and Table 1 show that the fused image based on Shearlets and PCNN keep better river information, and even involve excellent city features. In Fig 10.(d), in the middle of the fused image using Contourlet and PCNN, has obvious splicing effect. Fig.11(c) is the fused Hyperspectral image. Fig.11(a) and (b) are the two original images, The track of the airport is clear in Fig.11(a), however, some planes information are lost. Fig. 11(b) shows the different information. In the fused image, the track information is more clearly, and aircrafts characters are more obvious. But lines on the runways are not clear enough in the fused images using other methods. From Table 3 we can see that most metric values using the proposed method are better than other methods do.

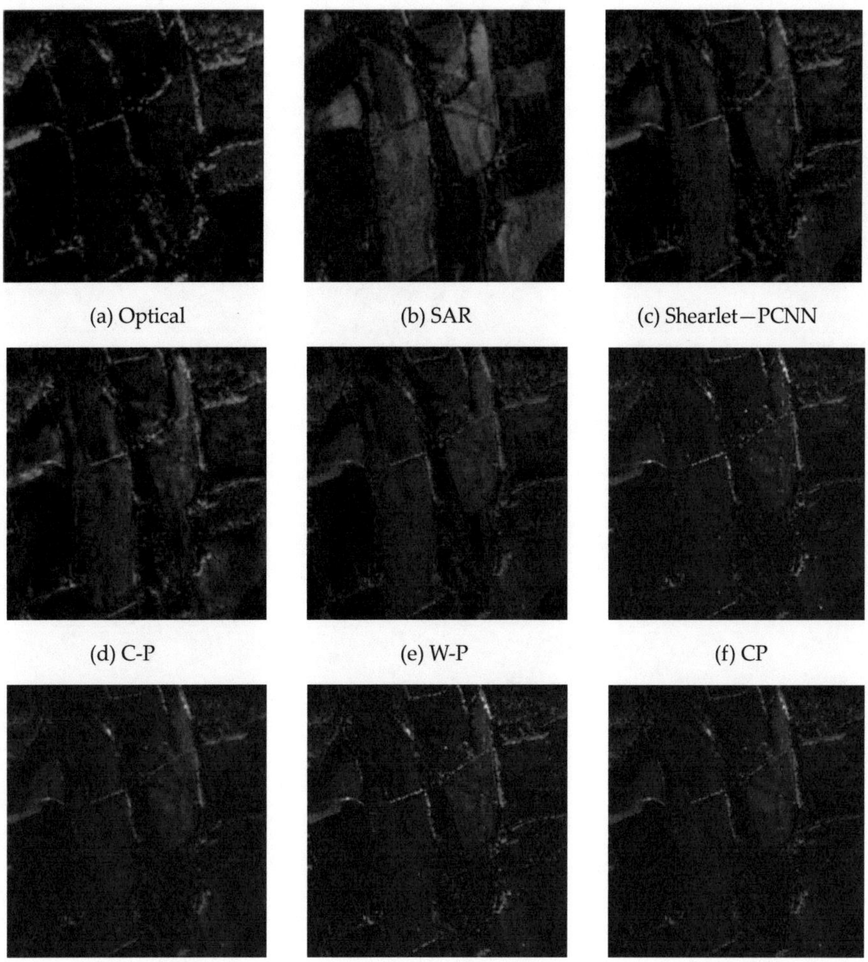

(a) Optical (b) SAR (c) Shearlet—PCNN

(d) C-P (e) W-P (f) CP

(g) Average (h) LP (i) GP

Figure 9. Optical and SAR images fusion results based on Shearlets and PCNN

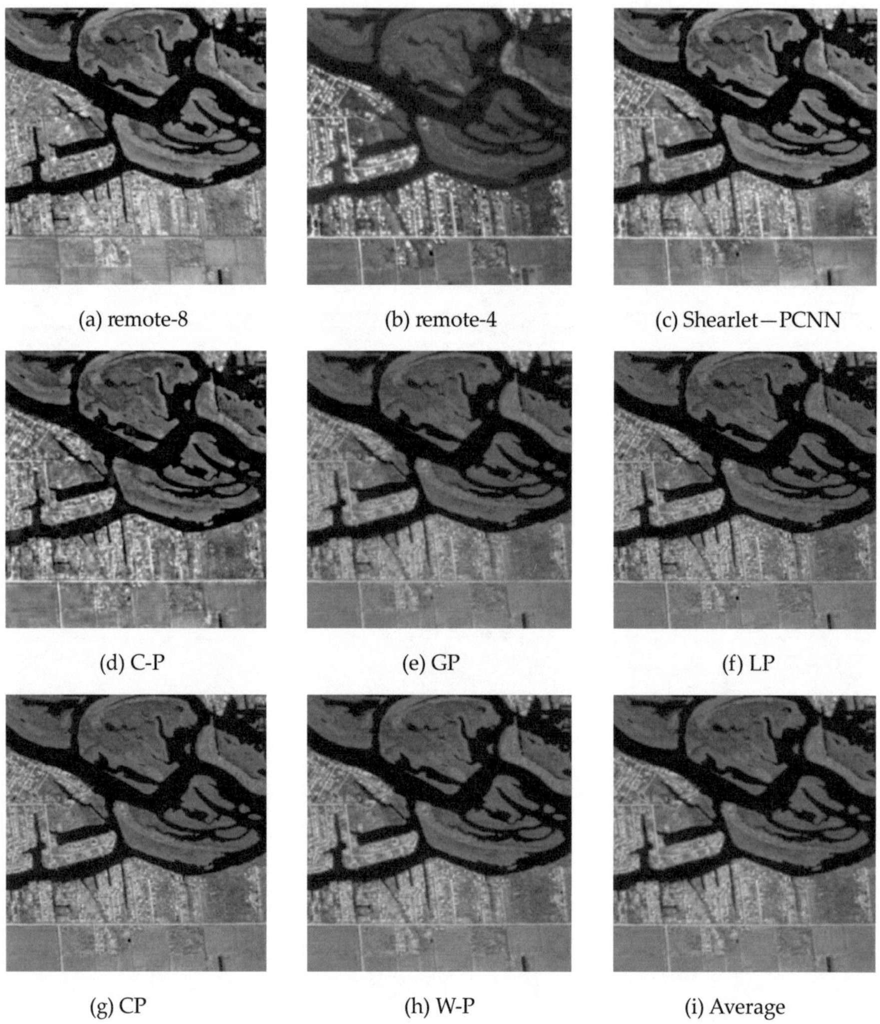

Figure 10. Remote sensing image fusion results based on Shearlets and PCNN

http://dx.doi.org/10.5772/56945

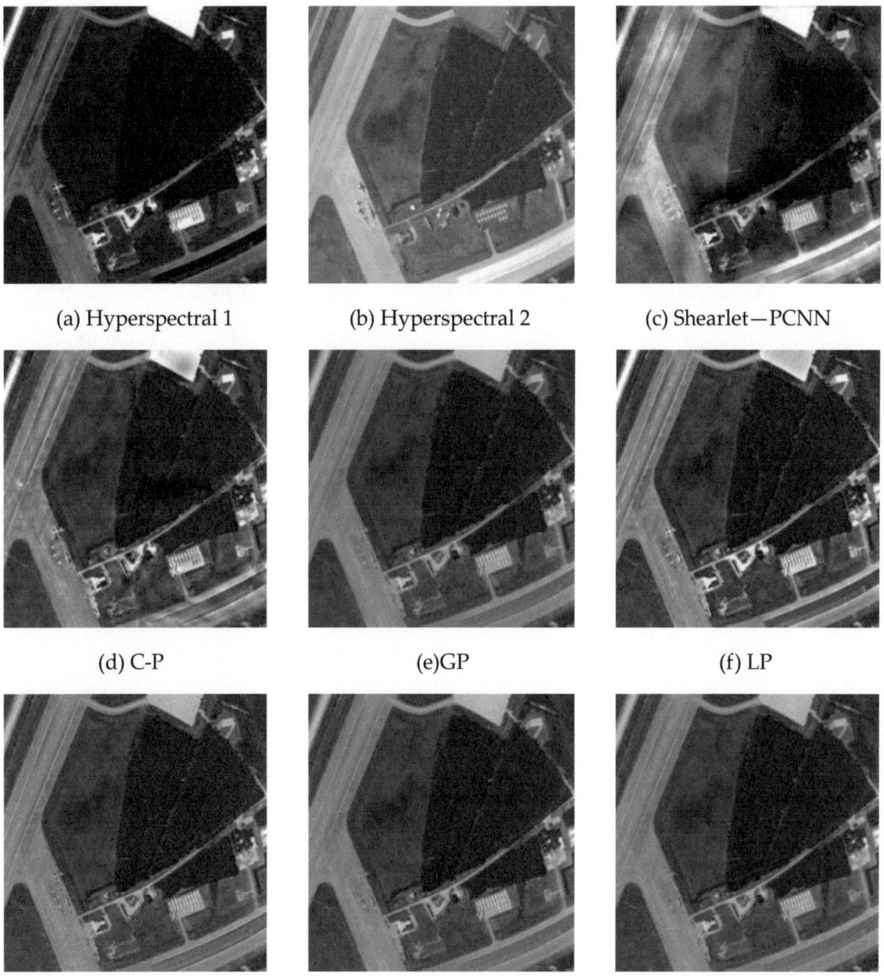

(a) Hyperspectral 1 (b) Hyperspectral 2 (c) Shearlet—PCNN

(d) C-P (e)GP (f) LP

(g) CP (h) W-P (i) Average

Figure 11. Hyperspectral image fusion results based on Shearlets and PCNN

Dataset	Algorithm	$Q_{AB/F}$	Q	EN	STD	Ave-grad	OCE
Experiment 1	Average	0.1842	0.2908	6.3620	22.1091	0.0285	3.2870
	LP	0.3002	0.3017	6.5209	24.8906	0.0478	3.0844
	GP	0.2412	0.2953	6.3993	22.6744	0.0379	3.2336
	CP	0.2816	0.2961	6.4759	24.1864	0.0457	3.1292
	C-P	0.3562	0.4523	6.7424	31.2693	0.0665	0.5538
	W-P	0.3753	0.4976	6.6142	25.2683	0.0662	0.5689
	proposed	0.4226	0.5010	6.9961	34.1192	0.0575	0.5410
Experiment 2	Average	0.4016	0.7581	6.1975	46.1587	0.0236	2.9600
	LP	0.5219	0.7530	6.9594	49.2283	0.0399	3.3738
	GP	0.4736	0.7599	6.9024	47.0888	0.0342	3.6190
	CP	0.5120	0.7475	6.9237	48.9839	0.0392	3.3812
	C-P	0.5658	0.7516	7.3332	54.3504	0.0390	3.0628
	W-P	0.4283	0.7547	6.8543	47.3304	0.0346	3.2436
	proposed	0.6212	0.7775	7.1572	56.2993	0.0381	2.9046
Experiment 3	Average	0.5021	0.7955	6.5011	41.0552	0.0161	1.0939
	LP	0.6414	0.7728	6.8883	47.4990	0.0274	0.9959
	GP	0.5720	0.7898	6.5649	41.3974	0.0223	1.0249
	CP	0.5909	0.7469	6.7499	43.4631	0.0318	0.9834
	C-P	0.5838	0.7435	6.9451	46.5294	0.0262	1.1745
	W-P	0.5319	0.7788	6.5847	41.6623	0.0231	1.5318
	proposed	0.6230	0.7502	7.0791	55.9533	0.0246	0.5246

Table 3. Comparison of image quality metrics

5. Conclusion

The theory of Shearlets is introduced in this chapter. As a novel MGA tool, shearlets offer more advantages over other MGA tools. The main advangtage of shearlets is that it can be studied within the framework of a generalized Multi-Resolution Analysis and with directional subdivision schemes generalizing those of traditional wavelets. This is very relevant for the development of fast algorithmic implementations of the many directional representation systems proved in the last decade.

In this chapter, we have succeed in demonstrations that shearlets are very competitive for-multi-focus image and remote sensing image fusion. As a new MGA tool, Shearlet is equipped with a rich mathematical structure similar to wavelet and can capture the information in any direction. And the edge and orientation information are more sensitive than gray according to human visibility. We take full advantage of multidirection of Shearlets and gradient information to fuse image. Moreover, PCNN is selected as a fusion rule to select the fusion coefficients. Because the character is tics of directional and gradient facilitate motivating PCNN neurons, the more precise image fusion results are gotten. Several different kinds of images, shown in the experiments, prove that the new algorithm we proposed in this chapter is effective.

After development in recent years, the theory of Shearlets is gradually improving. But the time complexity of Shearlets decomposition has been the focus of the study. Which need further study, especially in its theory and applications. We will focus on other image processing methods using shearlets in our future work.

Author details

Miao Qiguang, Shi Cheng and Li Weisheng

References

[1] S. G. Mallat, Theory for Multiresolution Signal Decomposition: The Wavelet Representation, IEEE Transaction on Pattern Analysis and Machine Intelligence, 11(1989),pp: 674-693.

[2] A. Krista, Z.Yun, D.Peter, Wavelet Based Image Fusion Techniques — An introduction, review and comparison, International Society for Photogrammetry and Sensing, 62(2007), pp: 249-263.

[3] J. P. Antoine, P. Carrette, R. Murenzi, B. Piette, Image Analysis with Two Dimensional Continuous Wavelet Transform. Signal Processing, 31(1993), pp: 241-272.

[4] F. G. Meyer, R. R. Coifman, Brushlets: A Tool for Directional Image Analysis and Image Compression. Applied and Computational Hamonic Analysis, 4(1997), pp: 147-187.

[5] N. Kingsbury, Complex Wavelets for Shift Invarian Analysis and Filtering of Signals. Applied and Computational Hamonic Analysis, 10(2001), pp: 234-253.

[6] P. Brémaud , Mathematical principles of signal processing: Fourier and wavelet Analysis, New York, 2002.

[7] Y. Xiao-Hui, J. Licheng, Fusion Algorithm for Remote Sensing Images Based on Nonsubsampled Contourlet Transform, Acta Automatica Sinica,34(2008), pp: 274-281.

[8] E. J. Candes, and D. L. Donoho, Continuous curvelet transform. I. Resolution of the wavefront set, Applied Computational Harmonic Analysis, 19 (2005), pp:162-197.

[9] M.N.Do, M.Vetterli, The Contourlet Transform: An Efficient Directional Multiresolution Image Representation, IEEE Transaction on Image Processing, 14(2005), pp: 2091-2106.

[10] M. QiGuang, W. BaoShu, Multi-Focus Image Fusion Based on Wavelet Transform and Local Energy, Computer Science, 35(2008), pp: 231-235.

[11] Wang-Q Lin, The Discrete Shearlet Transform: A New Directional Transform and Compactly supported Shearlet Frame, 5(2010), pp:1166-1180.

[12] G. Easley, Demetrio Labate and Wang-Q Lim, Sparse Directional Image Representations using the Discrete Shearlet Transform, Applied Computational Harmonic Analysis, 25(2008), pp: 25-46.

[13] G.Kutyniok. and D. Labate, Construction of Regular and Irregular Shearlet Frames, Journal of Wavelet Theory and Applications, 1(2007), pp: 1-10.

[14] G. Kutyniok and Wang-Q Lin, Image Separation Using Wavelets and Shearlets, Lecture Notes in Computer Science, 6920(2012), pp:416-430.

[15] K.Guo and D.Labate, Optimally Sparse Multidimensional Representation using Shearlets, SIAM Journal on Mathematical Analysis, 39(2007), pp: 298-318.

[16] G. Kutyniok and D. Labate, Resolution of the Wavefront Set using Continuous Shearlets, Trans. Amer. Math. Soc, 361(2009), pp:2719-2754. Shearlet webpage, http://www.shearlet.org.

[17] K. Guo, W. Lim, D. Labate, G. Weiss, E. Wilson. The theory of wavelets with composite dilations[J]. Harmonic Analysis and Applications. 4(2006), pp:231–249.

[18] K. Guo, W. Lim, D. Labate, G. Weiss, E. Wilson. Wavelets with composite dilations and their MRA properties[J]. Appl. Comput. Harmon. Anal.,20(2006), pp:231–249.

[19] K. Guo, D. Labate and W. Lim, Edge Analysis and Identification using the Continuous Shearlet Transform, Applied Computational Harmonic Analysis, 27(2009), pp: 24-46.

[20] G. Kutyniok and Wang-Q Lin, Image Separation Using Wavelets and Shearlets, Lecture Notes in Computer Science, 6920(2012), pp:416-430.

[21] K. Guo, W. Lim, D. Labate, G. Weiss, E. Wilson. Wavelets with composite dilations[J]. Electron. Res. Announc. Amer. Math. Soc., 10(2004), pp:78–87.

[22] R. Eckhorn, H. J. Reitboeck, M Arndt et al. Feature linking via synchronization among distributed assemblies: Simulation of results from cat cortex, Neural Computation, 2(1990), pp: 293-307.

[23] R. Eckhorn, H. J. Reitboeck, M Arndt et al. Feature linking via Stimulus-Evoked Oscillstions: Experimental Results form Cat Visual Cortex and Functional Implications form Network Model. In:Proc Int JCNN, Washington D C. 1(1989), pp:723-730.

[24] W. Jin, Z. J. Li, L. S. Wei, H. Zhen, The improvements of BP neural network learning algorithm, Signal Processing Proceedings ,2000, WCCC-ICSP 2000. 5th International Conference on, 3(2000),pp: 1647-1649.

[25] R. P. Broussard, S. K. Rogers, M. E. Oxley et al, Physiologically motivated image fusion for object detection using a pulse coupled neural network , IEEE Trans. Neural Network,10(1999), pp:554-563.

[26] W. Chen, L.C. Jiao, Adaptive tracking for periodically time-varying and nonlinearly parameterized systems using multilayer neural networks, IEEE Trans. on Neural Networks, 21(2010), pp:345-351.

[27] W. Chen, Z.Q. Zhang, Globally stable adaptive backstepping fuzzy control for output-feedback systems with unknown high-frequency gain sign, Fuzzy Sets and Systems, 161(2010), pp: 821-836.

[28] X.B.Qu, J.W.Yan, Image Fusion Algorithm Based on Features Motivated Multi-channel Pulse Coupled Neural Networks, Bioinformatics and Biomedical Engineering, 1(2008),pp: 2103-2106.

[29] X.B.Qu, C.W. Hu, J.W.Yan, Image Fusion Algorithm Based On Orientation Information Motivated Pulse Coupled Neural Networks, Intelligent Control and Automation, 1(2008),pp: 2437-2441.

[30] G.R. Easley, D. Labate, and F. Colonna, Shearlet Based Total Variation Diffusion for Denoising, IEEE Trans. Image Process. 18(2009),pp: 260-268.